THE CLASSIFIED CATALOG

THE CLASSIFIED CATALOG

BASIC PRINCIPLES AND PRACTICES

by

JESSE H. SHERA
Dean, School of Library Science
Western Reserve University

and

MARGARET E. EGAN
Research Associate, Center for Documentation
and Communication Research, School of Library
Science, Western Reserve University

With a Code for the Construction
and Maintenance of the Classified Catalog

by JEANNETTE M. LYNN, *Chief, Catalog Department*
and ZOLA HILTON, *Cataloger, The John Crerar*
Library

AMERICAN LIBRARY ASSOCIATION   CHICAGO, 1956

Foreword

In the bibliographical organization of research collections, the library catalog continues to serve a key role as an instrument for retrieval of information. It will continue to do so for as long as we can now see into the future.

The subject approach to library collections has been a problem of major concern to librarians for as far back as the records of librarians go. The attention given to the development of the subject catalog by the early founders of The John Crerar Library was therefore to be expected as one of the major fields of operation. The decision was made by the librarian-scientist, Clement W. Andrews, the Library's first administrator, to create a systematic subject catalog for the new library of science and technology. The system on which this systematic arrangement was based was the Dewey Decimal Classification.

By 1950 more than half a century of professional effort had gone into the production of a large and complex library catalog. That this was not an entirely satisfactory instrument for the purpose was probably as evident to the earlier reference librarians and catalogers at Crerar as it has been to the present staff. This is not to say that the catalog has not had a high degree of effectiveness.

The time came, however, when it was believed that some concerted effort should be devoted to the re-examination of the classified catalog to ascertain ways in which it might be improved. The staff was aware that there were many inconsistencies and deficiencies in the catalog. Various members of the staff, including reference librarians and catalogers, engaged in study and discussion of ways to bring about improvement. It was recognized early that a major deficiency was the lack of a manual to guide preparation and maintenance of the catalog.

A grant from the Rockefeller Foundation made it possible for us to undertake a project to fill this gap. This manual has resulted primarily from the scholarly approach to its preparation provided by the major authors, Dr. Shera and Miss Egan. It is their desire as well as ours that the manual be widely useful to other libraries as well as to The John Crerar Library. For this reason, it was prepared in a preliminary edition for review before publication and distributed to librarians representing a varied background of experience. They contributed numerous suggestions for improvement of the text, many of which were adopted.

It is a pleasure to acknowledge especially the assistance given by: Mrs. Pauline J. Love, Chief, Publishing Department of A.L.A., and a number of anonymous persons whom she consulted; Robert E. Moody, Director of Libraries, Boston University, and members of his staff; Miss Lucile M. Morsch, Deputy Chief Assistant Librarian, the Library of Congress; Floyd E. Orton, Science Librarian, State College of Washington (Pullman); Ralph H. Phelps, Director, Engineering Societies Library, and members of his staff; Dr. Maurice F. Tauber, Melvil Dewey Professor of Library Service, Columbia University, and his students; Elton Shell, Librarian, School of Religion, University of Southern California; and A. J. Wells, Editor, *The British National Bibliography*.

As might be expected, not all of the suggestions could be incorporated into the final text, partly because of conflict between suggestions and partly because of inconsistency with the purposes of the publication. For example, we could not leave out discussion of the theory of classification for one critic, and keep it in for another. It was kept in, and hereby hangs one of the principal criticisms of the manuscript. "The language is sometimes difficult to follow and unnecessarily complex" was a fairly moderate form of this criticism. The theory of classification does not make light reading in any book, as anyone who has read works on the subject referred to in this text can testify. So the reader who wishes to read theory of classification in monosyllables is strongly urged to skip Chapter 2. He will be a better classifier, however, if he does not.

Certain comments received arose out of a misunderstanding of the purposes of the book; these are clearly stated in the Preface. Interest was expressed in having included comparisons of costs between the classified catalog and the alphabetical subject catalog. This is an administrative problem only indirectly related to *how* to build and maintain a classified catalog. Some comparison of advantages and disadvantages between the two types of catalogs is ventured in Chapter 3, but these are largely empirical judgments. It is not the purpose of this little volume to "sell" the classified catalog. It is our serious hope that it will be useful to those libraries that decide to develop this type of catalog.

One of our correspondents wrote: "We are grateful for having been allowed to see this manuscript." It is we, kind sir, who should be and are deeply grateful for the patient and thoughtful attention given to the text by you and your fellow critics. It is, we trust, a better book because of you.

Herman H. Henkle
Librarian, The John Crerar Library

October 4, 1955

Preface

For many years the attention of librarians, particularly in the United States, has been devoted to promoting the *use* rather than the *organization* of library materials. The widespread adoption of the dictionary catalog and one of the two standard classification systems, the Dewey Decimal or the Library of Congress, seemed to have settled the major policies of organization. Library catalogs have always been subject to criticism as instruments for literature searching, but the size of older collections has made the costs of reclassification or recataloging too great to consider.

The twentieth century, however, has brought new pressures to bear upon the organizational processes of libraries and at the same time new opportunities to develop and test new methods in the many special libraries that have been established, particularly during and since World War II, to meet the new needs for intensive and thorough literature searching.

There has been, therefore, a renewal of interest in the classified catalog and a new burgeoning of enthusiasm for experimentation with new approaches to classification itself. Increasing specialization has made practicable and desirable the development of classification systems designed to cover certain limited subject fields, according to organizational patterns within the subject field itself, or adapted to a single operating situation.

There have been, in the United States, only four large classified catalogs, three of which are limited to science and technology, with the fourth being a general university catalog.[1] In view of the necessity for providing improved facilities for rapid location of precisely pertinent information, a re-examination of the qualities and potentialities of the classified catalog seems timely.

Because he believed that the classified catalog has important undeveloped potentialities for the organization of library materials, Herman H. Henkle, Librarian of The John Crerar Library, initiated a major re-examination of the classified catalog in relation to the collections, services, and clientele of Crerar Library. The present volume is one part of this undertaking.

Our mandate was to prepare a general manual for the classified catalog -- its functions, potential as well as realized, its characteristics, and the operating practices necessary to maintain its efficiency at the highest possible level. Our instructions were to impose upon the study no limitations as to classification system, particular collection, or even subject fields, although inevitably many of the ideas and much of the material has been drawn from the rich experience and seasoned judgment of those who have worked with the classified catalog at Crerar Library.

We have, therefore, attempted to attack the problem of the classified catalog through three stages: (1) the choice of the form of the subject catalog, (2) the choice of an appropriate classification system as the basis of organization, and (3) the procedures necessary for the construction and maintenance of the classified catalog. The first, last, and most important fact about the catalog is that it is not a machine. It is, rather, an instrumentality for objectifying and making permanent an *intellectual* process of analysis and synthesis. The success of any catalog depends ultimately upon the disciplined intelligence of those who plan and maintain it. For that reason constant attention has been given throughout this study to the intellectual processes which are fundamental in every phase of this problem.

Chapter 2 offers an introduction to the parts of formal logic that underlie classification. Grasp of the principles will be of material assistance to the classifier, yet readers who do not wish to undertake this discipline may readily omit Sections I-IV and go directly to Section V.

---

[1]Classified catalogs are maintained by The John Crerar Library in Chicago, the Engineering Societies Library in New York, the Science-Technology Department of the Carnegie Library of Pittsburgh, and Boston University Library.

The authors wish to acknowledge the very substantial assistance, the helpful suggestions, and enlightened criticism provided by Mr. Henkle and his Assistant Librarian, Miss Viola Gustafson.

Margaret E. Egan

Jesse H. Shera

Contents

Chapter 1

Nature and functions
of the library catalog

I. NATURE AND FUNCTIONS OF THE LIBRARY CATALOG

The library catalog does not--or should not--exist as an end in itself. It is one part of the total bibliographic system and must be responsive to changes that take place in other parts of the system. The history of the catalog has shown a certain degree of responsiveness to such changes under the impact of pressures stimulated by new needs or new resources. The modifications, however, have been unnecessarily slow, and sometimes inadequate, because of incomplete understanding of the nature and functions of the catalog and its place in the system as a whole.

The library catalog began as a simple inventory, or listing, of the contents of a particular collection. It may have been arranged alphabetically by author or title, topically by broad subject field, or merely according to position on the shelf, depending upon the particular librarian's concept of the chief purpose of the catalog. In an age when the volume of recorded literature remained so small that its resources could be known to every scholar, the only demand made upon the library catalog was that it show which items were in the particular collection.

As the volume of literature grew, both in bulk and in variety, new bibliographic devices were developed. John Boston de Bury's union list of manuscripts owned by English monastic libraries was merely an extension of the catalog of the individual library to include a group of libraries, indicating which one of many owned a particular title.[1] The early booksellers' lists carried the bibliographic process one step farther in that they indicated what titles were available, thus laying the foundations for our modern system of trade bibliography. To the booksellers also we may trace the initiation of certain of the descriptive functions of cataloging, such as size, number of pages, kind and condition of binding, price, and even some description of the contents, through listing the contents in cases of separate titles bound together, or through the arrangement of the catalog itself in broad subject categories for the benefit of the customer who might not know the author or title of a good book on the subject in which he was interested.

The first step toward universal bibliography was taken when Gesner compiled his ambitious world bibliography, the *Pandectarum sive Partitionum Universalium,* which included all the works he could discover arranged in some twenty-one subjects, regardless of availability in trade or in libraries. The rise to importance of the periodical eventually necessitated the preparation of indexes or other bibliographic guides to their contents. Thus the bibliographic system has grown, step by step, until today we have a very complex and not too well coordinated network of services, including trade and national bibliography, subject and biobibliography, individual library and union catalogs, periodical indexes, abstracting services, and compilations of bibliographic essays.

Until the last quarter of the nineteenth century the library catalog remained relatively untouched by these new developments. When in 1876 Cutter published his *Rules for a Printed Dictionary Catalog,* library catalogs generally were much the same as they had been for the past century. The advocates of the dictionary catalog sought to combine in one instrument the functions of several of the newer bibliographic tools. The merging of author, title, and subject entries in a single alphabet was held to be a tremendous step in simplification, but the dictionary catalog went even farther than this in including editor, compiler, translator, and illustrator

---

[1] "Cooperative Bibliography in the Thirteenth and Fifteenth Centuries" in: *Special Librarianship in General Libraries* (London: Grafton, 1939), pp.285-310. The earliest was the *Registrum librorum Angliae,* compiled by the Franciscans in the latter half of the thirteenth century. John Boston de Bury's *Catalogus scriptorum ecclesiae* was compiled early in the fifteenth century. Apparently there were many copies of the first because the second retained the same numbers to identify monastic libraries.

entries. The analytical entries indicating the contents of serials
or of sets of heterogeneous collected works tended to persist even
after new bibliographic instruments designed for this specific purpose became generally available. Thus the move toward simplification and economy eventually resulted in greater complexity and
costliness, until today librarians have begun seriously to question
the values of the dictionary catalog as a guide to materials in print.

At about the same time that enthusiasm for the dictionary catalog was running high in this country, librarians on the continent of
Europe were experimenting with the *catalogue raisonnée* or the
systematischer Katalog on the assumption that a classified catalog
is of greater utility to the scholar in that it brings together *related*
as well as *similar* materials. While the dictionary catalog, as its
name implies, derives from the modern dictionary, the adherents
of the classified catalog were no doubt influenced by the great systematic encyclopaedias of the eighteenth and nineteenth centuries.[2]

A. Objectives of the Catalog

Obviously, the idea that a library catalog can be so constructed
that it will serve every bibliographic need without the necessity for
recourse to other types of services is completely impracticable,
even if it were possible. Therefore, it becomes necessary to examine critically the functions that are most appropriate to the library
catalog in relation to those that are best carried out through other
instruments before discussing the principles and policies of the
catalog construction.

The functions that at one time or another have been delegated to
the catalog may be divided into two major categories, those related
to inventory and those related to retrieval, or location, of particular items within the collection.

Inventory

Though many of the early catalogs were little more than inven-
tories of the collections they represented, the modern library catalog is not organized to serve this end. The multiplicity of entries
needed for the effective operation of the catalog makes its use as
an inventory impracticable. Therefore the shelf list and the accession record are the proper instruments for inventory purposes,
though the latest practice strongly favors the elimination of the

---

[2]For an interesting discussion of the relative merits of the two systems of
arrangement, see Samuel Taylor Coleridge, *Treatise on Method*, ed. by Alice D.
Snyder, (London: Constable, 1934).

latter and the transfer of the information it contains to the shelf-
list card.

The use of the inventory as an aid to acquisition planning, though
it has been advocated by some writers, is not always an entirely
satisfactory procedure. In some parts of the collection it can be
quite useful as an aid in formulating the acquisition program but
the relative strengths and weaknesses of the several parts of the
collection can be more efficiently determined through the author
or subject catalog because the idiosyncrasies of the book arrangement may conceal rather than reveal the true nature of the collection.

Retrieval

Retrieval or location of particular items or groups of items is
certainly the most important function of the library catalog as we
know it today. One must emphasize, however, that this revelatory
process is limited in the catalog to materials available in the particular collection for which the catalog was prepared. Search beyond the confines of the immediate library necessitates the use of
such interlibrary mechanisms as union catalogs--national, regional,
or local; published union lists, such as the *Union List of Serials in
Libraries of the United States and Canada,* bibliographies which indicate libraries owning copies such as Evan's *American Bibliography,* Sabin's *Dictionary of Books Relating to America, The
London Bibliography of the Social Sciences;* and the interlibrary
loan process as described by Winchell's *Locating Books for Inter-
Library Loan.*[3]

The retrieval of material from the particular collection may be
accomplished through any one of a variety of points of access, each
of which has its own characteristic bibliographic device. These are
presented below in outline form:

Point of Access	*Bibliographic Device*
1. Knowledge of the identity of anyone instrumental in the production of the text	
a. Author: individual, corporate	Author entries in catalog of any type

---

[3]Constance M. Winchell, *Locating Books for Inter-Library Loan, with a Bibliography of Printed Aids which Show Location of Books in American Libraries*
(New York: Wilson, 1930).

Point of Access	Bibliographic Device
b. Illustrator	Added entry
c. Translator	Added entry
d. Editor	Added entry
e. Compiler	Added entry
f. In special fields, such others as composers, performers, etc.	Added entry
g. Publisher (Entries for publishers are not usually included in the card catalog except in those situations in which the publisher has the status of a corporate author.)	Trade bibliography: e.g., *Publishers Trade List Annual,* and lists of individual publishers
2. Knowledge of the title (Policy as to inclusion of title entries varies from library to library.)	Title entry in the author-title or dictionary catalog; bibliographies which include title entries such as trade, national, or subject bibliographies
3. Identification by form, physical or literary a. Encyclopedias b. Dictionaries c. Bibliographies d. Abstracting services e. Indexes f. Catalogs g. Directories	Identification by form may be accomplished through the form subdivisions used in conjunction with any subject heading, and in some instances through the form number of the classification schedule. Neither of these techniques, however, brings together all examples of a particular form. Form bibliographies are available for some of the types listed. A policy of physical segregation of certain types, usually encyclopedias, dictionaries, or bibliographies, is followed in many libraries.

Point of Access	*Bibliographic Device*
h. Maps and atlases	Specific policies with respect to the treatment of different forms will vary from one library to another according to needs. Such policies must be carefully formulated, recorded, and publicized. (See Chapter 2.)
i. Classification systems	
j. Nomenclatures	
k. Statistics	
l. History	
m. Biography	
n. Theory	
o. Fiction, belles-lettres	

4. Identification by time

    a. Period with which material deals — Period subdivisions of subject headings; classes for periods in classification schedule.

    b. Date of publication: original or edition — Chronological filing within classes, under subject headings, and under author or other secondary entry.

5. Identification by place

    a. Place discussed in text — Geographic subdivisions of subject headings, independent class in classification schedule, or subordinate schedule applicable to any class.

    b. Place of origin: text, edition, printer — National or special bibliographies; special catalogs of incunabula; histories of literature or of printing.

Point of Access	*Bibliographic Device*
6. Identification by language	
a. Original	National bibliographies; card catalog only when the subdivision *Books in . . . .* is used to indicate all books in a certain language owned by the library; special catalogs arranged by language.
b. Translations	Bibliographies of translations; language of the title on the catalog card indicates the language of the edition: the form subdivision *Translation* may be used, especially when there are many editions of a classic.
7. Physical features: binding, illumination, other decoration	Special bibliographies, or sections of special catalog of incunabula or other rare books.
8. By subject: selective, exhaustive	Catalog: Classified or the subject entries in an alphabetical arrangement. Subject bibliographies; indexes; abstracting services, etc. — the entire system for the subject analysis of recorded information.

This tabular presentation emphasizes five important generalizations:

1. *There is duplication, or at least partial duplication, of function between the library catalog and the other elements of the total bibliographic system.* There is further duplication within the other elements of the bibliographic system itself. Part of this duplication is both intentional and desirable. The small general library with limited holdings in a relatively large variety of fields will find the purchase of many of these bibliographic tools, however useful they may be, a financial impossibility. In such a situation the use of the library catalog as a substitute for such services is not wasteful duplication but an economically sound procedure. Likewise, the small but highly specialized library, designed to meet the needs of a

restricted clientele, may discover that the existing bibliographic
tools are, by their arrangement or organization, inappropriate.
Here too the use of a catalog especially constructed to meet local
needs is eminently justifiable even though the materials it covers
are duplicated in the more general services. In both of these situations, however, such uses of the library catalog create a bibliographic instrument the effectiveness of which is limited to the local
collection. In the small general library this limitation may not be
important, but in the specialized situation the catalog can hardly be
made to serve the purposes of conventional bibliographic mechanisms, however skilfully its organization is adjusted to local demands. Highly specialized needs are seldom limited to the resources of the local collection and hence the more general services
are necessary as guides to the resources beyond the limits of the
immediate collection.

Much of the duplication between the library catalog and the
other components of the bibliographic system is neither intentional
nor desirable. Often it is the result of pure inadvertence, a natural
consequence of isolated effort of several individuals working on the
catalog at various times, the product of inadequate coordination;
but it is also a characteristic of an age of transition in which local
responsibility for specific bibliographic services is being relin-
quished to centralized agencies for more general, and perhaps even
commercial, dissemination. Such duplication can, of course, take
many forms, e.g., the duplication represented by the history headings in the Library of Congress list with the history sections of
the classification schedules.

2. *There is a trend toward transfer of functions from the catalog to published bibliographic services.* The frequency with which
reference to published bibliographic services appears under "Bibliographic Device" indicates that there are available a considerable
number of services which analyze, according to patterns suitable to
most library needs, materials commonly found in a number of libraries. If this tendency toward centralized bibliographic analysis
continues it will have obvious effects upon the planning of the form
of future catalogs. One such effect will be to decrease the importance of local subject analysis and to increase the importance of
the catalog as a device for determining whether or not a particular
known item is locally available. This would seem to be a powerful
argument for the separation of author-title catalogs, which remain
relatively stable, from subject catalogs, the functions and characteristics of which vary greatly from place to place and from generation to generation.

3. *There has been too little consideration of the relative importance of the functions of the catalog.* The frequency with which the

catalog is mentioned, together with bibliographies, in relation to "Point of Access" indicates that the concept of universality of *function,* insofar as the collection cataloged is concerned, has tended to persist in cataloging practice. This concept has long been discredited among those who have given serious thought to the problems of bibliographic organization and the place of the catalog within the system. That many of these points of access are of secondary importance and might well be relegated to supplementary devices seems obvious. That certain others can be better and more economically served by other tools seems equally obvious. One of the primary tasks, therefore, in the planning of the catalog is a careful study of the importance of each of these approaches in the local situation, the evaluation of available bibliographic services, and the appropriateness of the catalog to meet those needs which are not otherwise serviced.

4. *Multiple functions of the catalog necessitate mixed principles of classification.* A corollary of the preceding generalization is that each of these points of access, or approaches, represents a different principle of classification and that to attempt to include all, or even several, of them in the catalog will inevitably result in a mixed classification system that is not effective in any respect. It would seem obvious, therefore, that to eliminate as many as possible of the approaches which are satisfactorily represented in other devices would simplify the problem of organizing the catalog, whether the pattern of arrangement is to be alphabetic or systematic.

5. *Finally, the catalog has two major functions.* The conclusion from both experience and analysis seems inescapable that there are two basic functions of the catalog that are of outstanding importance: (1) accurate and speedy determination of whether or not an item known by author or title is in the collection, and, if so, of where it may be found; and (2) what materials the library contains upon a given subject and where they may be found. It is with this second objective that the present work is concerned.

Retrieval Through the Subject Approach

The foregoing analysis of the functions of the catalog has brought us to the point of agreement that the most important function of the catalog is retrieval, and that retrieval through the subject approach is the most important aspect for those libraries most likely to be interested in using the classified catalog, and retrieval by subject is, of course, the *raison d'etre* of the classified catalog. This demands an intensive scrutiny of the specific objectives of the subject catalog, whatever its form.[4]

Theoretically, the objectives of any form of subject cataloging may be identified as follows:

1. To provide access by subject to *all* relevant material.

2. To provide subject access to materials through all suitable *principles of subject organization,* e.g., matter, process, applications, etc.

3. To bring together references to materials which treat of substantially the *same subject* regardless of disparities in terminology, disparities which may have resulted from national differences, differences among groups of subject specialists, and/or from the changing nature of the concepts with the discipline itself.

4. To show *affiliations among subject fields,* affiliations which may depend upon similarities of matter studied, of method, or of point of view, or upon use or application of knowledge.

5. To provide entry to any subject field at any *level of analysis,* from the most general to the most specific.

6. To provide entry through any *vocabulary* common to any considerable group of users, specialized or lay.

7. To provide a *formal description of the subject content* of any bibliographic unit in the most precise, or specific, terms possible, whether the description be in the form of a word or brief phrase or in the form of a class number or symbol.

8. To provide means for the user to make *selection* from among all items in any particular category, according to any chosen set of criteria such as: most thorough, most recent, most elementary, etc.

This list of objectives is a theoretical statement of what a subject catalog could, and possibly should, do if it could be developed without regard to limitations of personnel and finance. Practically, the objectives must always be modified to meet such limitations, but the necessary modifications should be the result of careful and well-informed consideration of (1) what objectives can be attained through other existing means even though they may entail a longer or more complicated process; (2) the relative costs of the means which are practicable alternatives; and (3) which objectives are essential, which are important and which are inconsequential to the group or groups which the library wishes to serve.

The first important policy decisions to be made in the planning of a catalog are:

1. Which objectives are to be adopted as indispensable and which are to be rejected as nonessential within the resources available?

---

[4]For a graphic presentation of the component elements of the catalog system see chart on page 67.

2. Given the particular objectives to be adopted, what is the best form of catalog for their realization?

3. What should be the relationship of the catalog to the other available bibliographic devices?

The first of these policy decisions is so closely geared to the particular situation and so much has already been said about objectives in general that little further discussion is appropriate here. A word of warning is in order, however, against the propensity to base such policy decisions upon casual observation, upon easy acceptance of professional traditions, or upon subjective opinion. Many more objective studies are needed of library use by particular groups, of the use of the same materials by different groups, of habitual patterns of literature searching on the part of such groups, and particularly of the relative effectiveness of such habits of search or of different bibliographic devices in disclosing all of the relevant material. Research projects of this type should result in the accumulation of a body of knowledge that would provide a substantial basis for many policy decisions, including those relating to objectives.

The best form of the subject catalog for any given situation poses a fundamental and often controversial problem. Growth in physical bulk and the extension of time required for searching have interfered seriously with the effectiveness of the present-day dictionary catalog. The complexities and intricacies involved in the use of the alphabetic arrangement may increase at a rate greater than the rate of physical growth, and if this proved to be true one would expect the alphabetic subject catalog to deteriorate eventually to a point at which other, and originally less effective devices, will begin to approach it in effectiveness.

It is this loss in effectiveness of the alphabetic subject catalog, and not a decrease in the need for a subject catalog, that has produced the growing dissatisfaction with the dictionary form. In general it may be said that as a collection grows in bulk and variety of subject matter, the need for an adequate subject catalog likewise increases, but the need for adequate subject coverage grows more rapidly than the volume of the collection. Further, as the need for a subject catalog increases, the need for a greater completeness of subject coverage also increases. But such a principle operates in opposition to the general belief of librarians that the subject catalog should be kept to a minimum, the implication being that library users prefer this. Actually, this practice is the result of the desire to keep down the size of the catalog so that its effectiveness will not decrease any more rapidly than is necessary. In other words, the difficulties of using a large dictionary catalog outweigh the advantages to be gained from more adequate subject coverage.

The first requisite, then, of any device for the subject analysis of bibliographic materials is that the rate of increase in the difficulties of its use remain of the same order of magnitude as that of its linear growth. With the expectation of indefinite subject catalog growth will come the definite possibility that the actual need for an adequate subject approach increases at an accelerating rate as the size of the collection grows, and concurrently there emerges the need for increased degree of subject coverage. The breaking point here must be controlled by the law of diminishing returns.

Similarly, the third set of decisions, those concerned with the relationship of the catalog to other bibliographic devices, are so intimately associated with local conditions that few general rules can be formulated. The following suggestions may prove helpful:

1. The ratio of the library's holdings to the listings in any bibliography bears an inverse relationship to the decision to analyze such materials in the library's own catalog. The patrons of a library which has only limited or popular resources in chemistry would find the use of *Chemical Abstracts* quite frustrating, unless the reader were prepared to make extensive use of photoduplication and interlibrary loan services.

2. It is the practice of most libraries to make subject cards for every monograph in the collection, even though some are included in standard published bibliographies, but to leave the close analysis of collections or journal literature to the standard services, such as *Psychological Abstracts*. When this is done, it is advisable to use cross references from all appropriate subjects to the bibliographic service.

3. General reminders to the user of the catalog that the catalog is supplemented by the special bibliographic tools will be helpful, and the bibliography collection should be shelved as close as possible to the catalog.

4. A good collection of standard indexes and abstracting services, with a visible index of the library's serial holdings and their location symbols, will in many cases obviate the necessity for any use of the catalog.

5. Expert professional assistance at the catalog and in the bibliography collection will ensure effective use of both and is essential in the procurement of materials which may be listed in a bibliography but which are not in the library's own collection.

B. Physical Forms of the Catalog

At this point, the crucial problem is the choice of an appropriate form for the subject catalog, and to this the remainder of this chapter will be devoted. The virtues of the card catalog are deeply ingrained in the thinking of librarians, although the recent decision of the Library of Congress to issue its author and subject catalogs in book form has again focused attention upon the peculiar advantages of this earlier practice. The development of electronic devices, on the other hand, has aroused speculation as to future possibilities for increasing the scope and flexibility of cataloging operations. A comparative analysis of time and cost factors made by Shaw,[5] however, indicates that the card catalog is not only far from obsolete but is in fact a remarkably efficient "machine." For most libraries, and certainly for small special libraries and libraries with relatively limited resources, the card catalog is the practicable choice as to physical form.[6]

Patterns of Arrangement

The well-known types of catalogs are: (1) alphabetic (which may or may not incorporate author and title files), (2) classed, and (3) alphabetico-classed.

The *alphabetic catalog* is so well known that it scarcely needs explanation. In it the arrangement is based on the accident of spelling, and when author entries, title entries, and subjects are combined in a single alphabet it is known as the dictionary catalog.

The *classed catalog,* by contrast, is necessarily limited to subjects, and in it the entries are arranged according to some preconceived scheme in which related subjects are brought together or associated each with the other.

The *alphabetico-classed catalog* is a hybrid form which attempts to combine the virtues of the two preceding types. It may assume either of two patterns: a catalog in which the subject entries are arranged alphabetically for the major divisions, with the subordinate groupings classified in an appropriate manner, or the major categories may follow a classified arrangement with the subordinate sections in alphabetic sequence. Its possibilities have never been adequately explored.

Not to be overlooked are the new experiments in multidimensional classification, which may require changes in the internal arrangement of classified catalogs but which does not constitute a separate type of catalog. Assuming for the present that one of the tested forms of card catalog is the most practicable choice, the

[5]Ralph R. Shaw, "Management, Machines, and the Bibliographic Problems of the Twentieth Century" in Chicago. University. Graduate Library School. *Bibliographic Organization* (Chicago: University of Chicago Press, 1951), pp.200-25.

[6]C. D. Gull, "Substitutes for the Card Catalog," *Library Trends,* v.2, no.2 (Oct. 1953), pp.318-29.

alternatives are usually considered to be the alphabetic or the
classed catalog.

There has been much debate over the relative merits of these
two systems. The greatest value of such debate for the present
purpose would seem to be that discussion from two points of view
helps to isolate problems that are inherent in an attempt to describe and group bibliographic units from problems that arise in
the process of arranging the resulting groups in logical order.
That is, such debate is helpful in enabling the classifier to distinguish the problems of bibliographic organization from the problems
of the organization of knowledge.

II. THE ALPHABETIC OR THE CLASSED CATALOG?

The user of the catalog always approaches the catalog with a
question which, in his mind, is formulated in words (verbalization
of a thought unit which may or may not correspond to any existing
bibliographic unit). This verbal formulation must be translated
into the formal categories of the catalog, whether these categories
are labeled verbally or nonverbally.

In the case of the classified catalog, the user's verbalization is
converted into the terminology of the catalog through the use of:

1. The classification schedule.

2. The subject index to the classed catalog, which gives the
    class number attached to the word or phrase used as the
    subject heading.

3. Other visual aids: charts, diagrams, etc., which reproduce
    appropriate sections of the classification schedule and are
    displayed in close proximity to the part of the catalog to
    which they refer.

4. His own partial, and possibly inaccurate, memory of class
    numbers he has used on previous occasions.

5. Personal assistance of the professional librarian.

In the case of the alphabetic catalog, there may be sufficient
correspondence, in terminology, precision, and specificity, between
the vocabulary of the user and that of the catalog so that the user
goes directly to the subject heading under which he will find relevant titles. If not, either he must try a different term or he must
follow a cross reference which directs him to the proper place.

This latter procedure is exactly equivalent to using the subject index to the classified catalog, which is in effect a separate file of cross references.

In both types of catalog, the reader will be referred to related fields which may or may not be contiguous. In the dictionary catalog, the method of referral will always be the separate card for cross reference and the referral will be to a heading in the alphabetic file isolated by an accident of spelling. In the classed catalog, referral may take place through two methods:

1. Additional numbers, representing separate aspects of the subject, on the index card.

2. Adjacency of related classes, both more general and more specific, in the catalog itself.

If, then, the first step in the processing of materials is the same for both catalogs, i.e., the accurate description of each bibliographic unit and the grouping of similar units under some formal designation descriptive of the group, then the chief differences are those of the order of arrangement of the groups (classes) and the system of symbols used to designate them.

The apposition of the alphabetic catalog to the classed catalog on this basis is not completely justified. Both require the basic steps in classification and differ only in the arrangement of the resulting classes. But even at this stage, there is not a true dichotomy, for each partakes somewhat of the nature of the other; the alphabetic catalog is fundamentally a concealed classification, and throughout it makes use of the principles of classification:

1. By the use of inverted and compound headings which assemble related materials without reference to the alphabet.

2. By the use of an elaborate system of cross references (integrated by means of tracings) which guide the user to related materials, otherwise dispersed throughout the alphabet.

Conversely, the classified catalog may at times introduce the principle of alphabetic arrangement when more strictly logical principles do not apply or are not practically expedient. Both may make some use of chronologic arrangement. The extent of difference between the classed and the alphabetic catalog depends upon the extent to which each adheres to its own basic principle of organization; the two types merge in the alphabetico-classed catalog.

A discussion of the alleged advantages and disadvantages of the two types will serve to clarify the later discussion of the reasoning underlying the recommendation of certain general principles or particular rules for the construction and maintenance of the classified catalog.

A. The Alphabetic Subject Catalog

Advantages

1. Order of the alphabet is common knowledge and is constantly used in other situations.

2. Directness of access: reader is likely (although not certain) to find references under the word or phrases he chooses to consult first.

3. The verbal headings used in place of code symbols are probably more easily understood and impose fewer psychological obstacles to the average user.

4. Greater freedom in the introduction of new groupings, inasmuch as groups of materials gathered together under a descriptive verbal heading need not bear the same logical relationship one to another that the classes in a systematic classification must maintain.

5. Opportunity to consolidate author-title and subject catalogs into one file has been generally assumed to be an advantage, but this may be questioned since such a combination results in increasing complexity as the catalog grows in size. Furthermore, such consolidation confuses two separate and often unrelated functions of the catalog.

Disadvantages

1. Excessive dependence upon verbalization.

a. Multilingual use is difficult: no possibility of international standardization and minimal possibility of international cooperation.

b. Rapid obsolescence of verbal terms in some fields.

    c. Regional, or social-group, variations in terms for the same concept.

    d. Use of same term in more than one meaning, or with subtle shades of difference in meaning.

    e. Underlying principle of classification obscured by alphabetic dispersion, resulting in
      (1) Inconsistencies in applying principles of classification.
      (2) Possibility of unintentional dispersion of materials through use of synonyms or near-synonyms.

    f. Necessity for some artificial and arbitrary decisions about definitions, thus confusing readers, whose individual interpretations may be at variance with those of the catalog.

    g. Verbal headings forced to serve a dual function:
      (1) As index entries--a finding device.
      (2) As device for grouping related subject entries.

    h. Because of this dual role, subject headings in the alphabetic catalog must be more complex than entries in the index to a classified catalog.

    i. General weaknesses of subject headings *per se*--at least in the present state of the art. A true "philosophy" of subject headings still remains to be developed.

2. Growth of the catalog, especially in large research libraries, results in increasing complexity, which, in turn, necessitates the formulation of an elaborate code of practice, not only for differentiation among the several types of entry but also for the mechanics of filing. The applications of this code are often unfamiliar to even the most experienced users of the catalog.

3. The interfiling of a variety of types of entry in one alphabet may be seriously confusing to the user. This confusion is especially apparent in the failure of many users to distinguish between title and subject entries. This is especially true in those instances in which the title resembles a plausible subject heading and hence is assumed to represent the entire holdings of the library for that particular topic. Differentiation in typography conveys little or no meaning to the nonlibrarian.

4. The interfiling of author, title, and subject entries in the dictionary catalog confuses two functions, or more precisely, two types of demands made upon the catalog. The relation between this and "Advantage 5" is very close. Often the line of demarcation is almost indistinguishable.

One should remember, of course, that the alphabetic catalog is not necessarily a dictionary catalog, though in the United States they are generally understood as being synonymous. The last two criticisms, therefore, apply only to the dictionary type and would be obviated in the divided catalog in which author-title and subject entries are filed in separate alphabets.

B. The Classified Catalog

Advantages

1. Notational system independent of language.

    a. Possibility of international standardization and hence cooperation.

    b. Changes in terminology (or differences among groups) do not necessitate recataloging--only index cards need be revised. Any explanatory notes needed may be added to the index card from which the user obtains the class number, whereas in the dictionary catalog such explanations cannot appear on each card bearing the subject headings.

    c. Synonyms, or near-synonyms, may occur in index, referring to the same class number, without dispersing the references.

    d. Classes have explicitly defined scope and content, delineated in part by their place in the hierarchy as well as by verbal definitions.

2. Diminution of language barriers through the use of an arrangement that depends for its effectiveness upon logical relationships rather than linguistic association. The director of the newly established National Library of Canada has announced the establishment of a classified catalog organized by the Library of Congress classification instead of the more traditional dictionary catalog. This choice was due almost entirely to the fact that the Canadian population is bilingual.

3. Closely related classes are brought together in sequence, where they may be scanned for materials slightly more general or more specific than the class directly referred to. Thus it stimulates use of additional materials. Alphabetic subject catalog satisfies conscious needs of readers but classed catalog stimulates hitherto unrealized needs.

4. Stimulates multidimensional approach. ("Only the classed catalog provides one with the advantages of thorough exploration of a given field both vertically... and horizontally..."[7] and, one might add, tangentially.)

5. Offers opportunity for interpolation of special classification systems in certain fields.[8]

6. Permits easy compilation of bibliographies through reproduction of specified sections of the catalog.

7. For exhaustive literature searching the classified catalog offers great assurance that all possibilities have been explored. Display of logically related fields facilitates checking all approaches.

8. Facilitates (although it does not insure) consistency in application of principles of classification.

9. The classed catalog may form a bridge between bibliothecal arrangement and the classification of knowledge itself. In assigning subject headings to a book the cataloger begins with the particular book and searches the list of subject headings for terms which seem to him best suited to the description of its contents; in contrast, the user of the book begins with the subject and inquires of the catalog what titles are related to his purposes. The point of view of the classifier more nearly resembles that of the user since he is concerned with the relation of the book to an entire subject field.

10. The classed catalog, by forcing the separation of the author-title and the subject files, emphasizes the distinction between the function of these two major tools.

[7]Arthur B. Berthold, "Future of the Catalog in Research Libraries," *College and Research Libraries*, VIII (Jan. 1947),pp.20-22.

[8]Jeannette M. Lynn, "Future of Cataloging and Classification," *Catholic Library World*, XIII (Feb. 1942), pp.138-44.

11. Index to classified catalog easier to use than complex system of subject entries in alphabetic catalog.

12. Use of subject index to classified catalog may be an actual time saver, and in addition it can be a supplement to the classified catalog by introducing dimensions which cannot be brought out by the classification scheme.

Disadvantages

1. Order of arrangement is not a matter of common knowledge, as alphabet is.

2. Necessity for use of the subject index to the classification system introduces a second step which may not be necessary in the more direct approach to the alphabetic catalog.

3. When the system of organization within a subject field is overthrown by advancing knowledge, the entire section of the classification system dealing with that subject becomes obsolete. This may be true of a minor class or even of one of the major classes. Revision of a single subject field is difficult because of the many interrelations with coordinate classes.

4. The notational system of the classified catalog creates an impression of intricacy which may impose a psychological barrier to effective use.

5. Critics of the classed catalog have claimed that users of the catalog do not want a complete survey of the field, but prefer the quickest possible reference to a specific point or item. This criticism overlooks the fact that the user of the classed catalog may go to a single and quite specific point of reference, ignoring the adjacent classes completely.

6. The tendency of classified catalogs to be based upon traditional library classification systems which are themselves illogical or already obsolete is often mentioned as a criticism. This is not a weakness inherent in the classified catalog itself, but is rather a criticism of the particular choice of a classification system as the basis of the catalog. Many librarians, finding existing systems unsuitable to their purposes, have constructed special classifications, just as many have developed their own systems of subject headings. Furthermore, although traditional library systems are based upon the actual

handling of collections of monographic literature and were
originally intended for the physical arrangement of the books
on the shelves, it is not necessary--and perhaps not desira-
ble--for the classification system used in the classified catalog to be the same as that used for shelf arrangement and
thereby subjected to the limitations of linear arrangement of
physical objects.

The decision to adopt one type of catalog in preference to the
other is not an obvious one. The fact that the arguments favoring
the classified catalog outnumber those supporting the alphabetic arrangement does not necessarily argue for the superiority of the
former in all situations. The arguments must be weighted in terms
of individual needs, and in some libraries simplicity may be the
sole consideration. But what values may be assigned to these
weights, and what arguments take precedence over others in particular situations cannot here be specifically stated, or even general-
ized. In actual practice it may develop that the decision to adopt
one form of catalog in preference to another may not be too difficult
if one knows what is to be expected of it. But what is to be expected
of the catalog? How does its use differ in varying libraries? Is
the alphabetic catalog really "best" in the public library? Answers
to such questions must of necessity wait upon the findings of an extensive program of research similar to that described in the con-
cluding chapter.

Chapter 2

General principles
for the construction
of a classification system

INTRODUCTION

The central factor in the success or failure of a classified catalog is the efficacy of the system of classification upon which the
catalog is based. This would seem to be a truism but it has been
consistently ignored in previous treatments of the subject, primarily
because their authors have assumed the use of one of the standard
bibliothecal schematisms such as that of Dewey or, more commonly,
the Universal Decimal System, which is based upon Dewey's work.
There is a substantial body of criticism, both theoretical and practical, of the Dewey classification, most of which applies with equal
force to the Universal Decimal System. While many of the arguments are undeniably valid, it is unfortunate that such criticism
has been permitted to weigh against the utility of the classified catalog itself. There has been almost no attempt to evaluate the usefulness of the classified catalog when the classification upon which
it is based is well designed for its purpose.

There are available many classification systems other than the
well-known standardized bibliothecal systems, and an increasing
number of librarians are experimenting with the construction of

special systems designed to fit their local needs. The first principle to be remembered in either choosing or constructing a classification is that there is no single universal system that will serve all purposes in all fields. The second principle is that there are no absolute values in classification other than those of utility in the particular situation. A classification system is not an arbitrary or an abstract structure; it is, in a very real sense, a function of the interaction between characteristics of the material to be organized and the expected patterns of use of the material. This is true of bibliothecal classifications as well as of the scientific classifications within the several fields of knowledge.

The librarian who wishes to experiment with classification or to make intelligent decisions within the framework of one of the standard systems must be well informed in five general areas:

1. The principles of classification derived from traditional logic

2. Special problems arising in bibliothecal classification.

3. The characteristics and structure of the body of literature to be classified.

4. The patterns of recourse to the literature which are habitual to the major group of users.

5. Local conditions which affect administrative decisions with respect to the catalog.

It is the purpose of this chapter to provide a general introduction to these five areas, in the hope that the interested librarian will be encouraged to read and to explore further, particularly in the less known areas, and perhaps eventually add to our admittedly sparse knowledge of some of these factors.

I. PHILOSOPHICAL PRINCIPLES OF CLASSIFICATION[1]

Despite the denial of absolute values in classification, the

---

[1]This section leans heavily upon the following references, specific citations being given when an exact definition is borrowed or a passage closely paraphrased:

Henry E. Bliss, *The Organization of Knowledge and the System of the Sciences* (New York: Henry Holt, 1929).

A. Broadfield, *The Philosophy of Classification* (London: Grafton, 1946).

M. R. Cohen and Ernest Nagel, *An Introduction to Logic and Scientific Method* (New York: Harcourt Brace, 1934).

R. N. Piper and P. W. Ward, *The Fields and Methods of Knowledge* (New York: Alfred Knopf, F. S. Crofts, 1929).

W. C. Berwick Sayers, *A Manual of Classification for Librarians and Bibliographers*, 2d ed. rev. (London: Grafton, 1944).

history of the theory of classification is largely the narrative of a succession of searches for absolutes or universals. The quest of the great philosophers for a single classification of all knowledge may be rejected, without sacrificing the contribution they have made in isolating and defining the abstract categories or principles which may be flexibly applied in different ways to different bodies of material. The major concepts that have been so isolated and defined are still valuable even in the newer approaches to classification, and a brief summary of the principles derived from this main stream of logical theory is fundamental to a better understanding of bibliothecal classification.

A. Basic Concepts

No theory of knowledge, and therefore no ordering of knowledge, is possible without taking into account the inherent ability of the human mind to form concepts, and to perceive beyond *concepts* the fundamental *categories* which pervade and organize the almost infinite number of possible specific concepts. Because classificatory processes of every kind are dependent upon this inherent intellectual ability, the classifier must begin with an explicit understanding of *concept* and *category*.

Concept

The term *concept* has initiated many a doctrinal dispute among philosophers. Differences of opinion have arisen mostly over the nature of the mental image, the percept, and the concept, and the relation of each to the external world, or "reality." With these disputes we need not be too much concerned. If we accept the definition that a concept is the recognition of a pattern of qualities, or a structure, which enables the mind to name the object in reality with recurrent consistency, we shall avoid the doctrinal disagreement and have a good working basis for our own immediate purpose. A concept, therefore, may refer to a particular instance--Mr. Brown, our own dining table, the saving of a life--or it may through a progressive discarding of the particularizing qualities ascend to higher levels of generality--man, domestic furnishings, heroism.

Different fields of knowledge or of activity focus attention upon different points in the ascending scale of generality. This is one of the facts which makes any universal scheme of classification unwieldy for most special purposes, thereby giving rise to the multitude of special classification systems, each of which focuses upon the level of generality or particularity which is fundamental in its own frame of reference. The *unit of thought,* or the *information*

unit, is always relative to a particular frame of reference and must
be identified within that frame. By building special classification
systems around such identified units, at an appropriate level of conceptualization, it is possible to ignore concepts or classes which
fall above, below, or completely outside, the established field.

The best statement concerning levels of conceptualization has
been made by Giddings:

> "The particular instance of something or other which has ar-
> rested our attention looks like a unit or item, detached or de-
> tachable, and so we think of it for the moment. Then we make
> further discoveries. Our instance is a unit as far as its rela-
> tions with other instances like itself or different happen to go,
> but if we leave them out of our field of vision and forget them,
> and look intently at our particular instance we see it resolve
> into a multitude of lesser items, arranged perhaps in clusters
> or patterns, and, like enough, moving about. Each of these items
> in turn, we presently ascertain, is composite, and so on, without
> end.

> "Human society abounds in examples and the social worker
> encounters them. He may be interested chiefly in a mill town,
> or chiefly in a neighborhood, or chiefly in certain families. At
> one time he will be most concerned about what the mill town or
> the neighborhood or a family does. At another time he will be
> most concerned about what it is. As long as he is attending to
> what the mill town does he thinks of it as a whole. It is a com-
> munity. He compares it with other communities as wholes. He
> observes similarities and differences of activity and achieve-
> ment. These observations may lead him to ask why such simi-
> larities and differences exist, how they are to be accounted for.
> Trying to answer this question, he finds himself inquiring what
> his mill town is, and from that moment he is resolving it into
> components. He is discovering that it is made up of corpora-
> tions, trade unions, churches, schools, shops and markets, pro-
> fessional men and business men, skilled mechanics and unskilled
> labourers, native born folk and foreign born folk of various na-
> tionalities; in fine, of inhabitants arranged in bewildering clus-
> ters and patterns. If he is interested chiefly in a neighborhood
> or in a family he has a like experience. He thinks of it as a unit
> while he is learning what it does. He necessarily thinks of it as
> a composite when he tries to learn what it is.

> "A particular instance, then, is a unit or not as we happen,
> or have occasion, to see it, and we have occasion to see it in the

one or the other way according to the nature of the investigation that we attempt to make. If it is our purpose to learn how our particular instance is related to other instances like itself, or behaves toward them or with them, or enters into a combination with them to make up a bigger whole; or how it is related to things (that is to say instances) unlike itself, and behaves toward them or with them, or enters into combination with them — our instance is a unit, and we deal with it as such. But if our purpose is to learn what it *is,* if we are attempting to account for it, and to understand it, our unit of investigation must obviously be an item of lower order. Practically it must be an item of the next lower order. In accounting for things we must go back step by step." [2]

Category

A *category* is a concept in the sense in which concept has just been defined. Like any other generic concept it refers to the totality of items embraced under the concept. Thus the category of existence is the concept of existent things; the category of quality is the class of all qualities. The category is related referentially to its instances, precisely as the ordinary class concept "man" is related to Smith, Brown, Jones, and other individual men. But, it may be objected, "If a category *is* a concept, what distinguishes a category from a noncategorical concept? What is the place of the categories in the scheme of concepts?" A categorical concept differs from any other generic concept solely in its comprehensiveness and generality. *A category, conceptualistically defined, is then a concept of high generality and wide application.* Or it may be defined as the most general kind of existence or reality which any mentionable object can have. When the thought content of any term whatever has been referred back to, or placed under, its proper category, thinking about that particular thought content has reached its culmination.

Categories are the indispensable cohesive elements in all thinking processes. Analysis at any level brings to light certain "field ideas" that constitute the background of all thought, and long before the individual is conscious of these ideas as facts in themselves he is using them in his thinking. In short, one thinks *with* categories long before he thinks *about* them. It is one of the concerns of logic to bring these "field ideas" to light, to isolate them and to identify them as "categories" so that they can be made objects of study in

[2]F. H. Giddings, "The Scientific Scrutiny of Societal Facts" in: V. F. Calverton, ed., *The Making of Society* (New York: The Modern Library, 1937), pp.613-15.

themselves and useful instruments in any process of classification.

The categories, since they differ only in generality from other class concepts, are arrived at by progressive generalization of concepts.

While a categorical concept refers primarily to the multiple instances of the concept, each category also envisages a unitary character which supposedly pervades the many exemplifications of the categories. Thus the category of existence is conceived to be a peculiar mode of being which spreads itself "over" or "under" all existent things. The category of quality is a unique determination of all actual qualities.

The eliciting of the categories from experience is not always a simple process of abstraction and generalization. A sensuous category, like quality, is attained by ascending from particular attributes to generic concepts, like red — color — etc., and finally to quality itself as a summum genus. But the less sensuous categories, like thinghood or possibility, are the products of creative and constructional activities of thought in addition to mere abstraction and generalization. Such constructional categories are distinctly pragmatic in their origin and function, having been devised by the human mind to cope more effectively with the experiential order than is possible by abstraction alone. But however far removed the nonsensuous categories may seem to be from the "given," they are not spun out of thin air in utter disregard of the nature of experience but are in every case suggested by experience and derive their meaning from indirect reference to that which is experientially given.

Although experience perhaps suggests a certain categorical system, it does not uniquely determine a given set of categories so that it and no other is coercive. Alternative categorical schemes may be devised for the interpretation of experience, just as alternative geometrics or alternative logics may be, and the choice of a certain scheme in preference to its rivals is dictated solely by its greater success in integrating and organizing the experiential data from which every scheme of categories ultimately derives.[3]

Aristotelian Categories. Aristotle used the term *category* to express the ten classes of being, or the typical forms of speech used to express being, or, finally, the typical judgments regarding being. The Aristotelian categories were:

---

[3]For fuller discussion of the concept of "category," see Ledger Wood, *The Analysis of Knowledge* (London: Allen and Unwin, 1940), pp.147-50.

1. Substance

2. Quantity

3. Quality

4. Relation (especially such as double, half, greater than, etc.)

5. Place

6. Time

7. Situation or position (such as is expressed by *to sit* or *to lie*)

8. Possession of acquired character (such as dress or ornament)

9. Activity (in the more special sense such as is expressed by active verbs like *to cut* or *to burn*)

10. Passivity or passion (such as is expressed by the passive voice of any active verb)

Kant's Categories. Kant revised the categories of Aristotle to make them dependent upon the forms of judgment. These forms of judgment involved the fundamental ways of thinking of objects, and his table of categories is, therefore, explicitly a classification of the possible objects of human thought according to the fundamental ways in which the human mind can conceive or understand objects. The categories of Kant were:

1. Categories of quantity
   Unity
   Plurality
   Universality

2. Categories of quality
   Reality
   Negation
   Limitation

3. Categories of relation
   Substantiality
   Causality
   Reciprocity

4. Categories of modality
   Possibility
   Actuality
   Necessity

Ranganathan's Fundamental Categories. These modes of being, as identified first by Aristotle and refined and reclassified by Kant, must have been at least vaguely operative in the minds of the authors of the Universal Decimal Classification when they added to their expansion and modification of the Dewey system certain supplementary signs or symbols of association and relationship. These associational devices often paralleled the Aristotelian modes of being — time, place, point of view, relation, etc.

However, it remained for S. R. Ranganathan to develop fully the application of this Aristotelian principle to the analysis of the structure of recorded information. In devising his Colon Classification, Ranganathan identified four major ways in which knowledge itself grows and ejects new areas of knowledge or specific subjects. These four methods are:

1. Denudation
   Which results in subordinate classes, or chain of classes

2. Dissection
   Which results in coordinate classes, or array of classes

3. Lamination
   Which results in composite classes

4. Loose-assemblage
   Which results in combination classes

From this understanding of the way in which knowledge increases, and its influence upon the structural pattern of a classification, it became possible for Ranganathan to identify a variety of "facets," or aspects of relationships which the constituent parts of all knowledge bear to each other. This variety of facets he was eventually able to classify into the five fundamental categories:

1. Time

2. Space

3. Energy or action

4. Matter

5. Personality

These are, in effect, Aristotelian modes of being, in terms of which any mental concept may be expressed.

Names (Terms)

If the formation of concepts is the first step in any thought process, the next step, or perhaps the final phase of conceptualization, is the act of naming. Without names there could be no transmission of concepts from one mind to another. The act of naming begins with a given content and elaborates it into an intelligible thought system or inferential unit. Even a single idea, or name, is a complex or inferential whole — an implicative system at a given level of generality.

In the very first stages of knowledge the mental processes are engaged in distinguishing definite objects, qualities, or relations, ordering them into a system, and identifying this system with some linguistic element, for all others as well as for the individual engaged in the intellectual act, until at some future time that word, or name, or symbol, stands for or "means" that specific implicative system and no other.

Names, then, viewed as distinct from the act of naming, may be defined as words, groups of words, or symbols used to designate a definite meaning or an inferential whole. In the view of Aristotle, a name, when first given, may be a mere convention, but one must observe William James's caution that, though names may be arbitrary, once they are understood and accepted, they must be adhered to.

In a single assertion or judgment many different names may occur, but as understood by the logician all of these may be reduced to two classes, the *subject* and the *predicate*, and these are known as the "logical terms."

A classification is expressed in class *names* or *terms*, which are the verbal correlate of the class each denotes, and which may be a single word or phrase which expresses adequately the connotation of the class for which it stands.[4]

They are briefer than definitions, more definite than signs or symbols. They are used to designate, not to define. That which they designate the definition makes explicit, though in the absence of a standardized and precise nomenclature the name may partake of the character of a definition.[5]

Terms should be used with consistent meaning throughout any one classification scheme and ideally throughout every act of classification.

Terms should never be ambiguous. They may be either technical or popular, depending upon the anticipated use of the classification. General preference for the technical is perhaps prompted by the belief that it is likely to be more permanent, less ambiguous and more widely understood.

---

[4]Berwick Sayers, *op. cit.*, p.80.
[5]Bliss, *op. cit.*, pp.138-39.

Definition

The relation between classification and definition has never been
quite adequately described. In a sense, it is a circular relationship,
for both are techniques for the systematic analysis and orderly description of phenomena. Classification must begin with the explicit
analysis of that which is to be classed — the essence of definition —
while definition delineates the classes within the hierarchy of the
classification.

A *definition* may be described linguistically as a proposition, or
fact statement, in which the subject is the exact equivalent of the
predicate, one term being *denotative* and the other *connotative*.
The denotative term indicates the *extension,* while the connotative
indicates the *intension* of the phenomena being defined.

Definition may take a variety of forms, usually depending upon
the nature of the matter to be defined or upon the purpose for which
the definition is to be used. The most familiar forms of acceptable
definition are:

Logical definition, in which the object or concept to be defined
is referred to its proximate genus (the next higher class in an established hierarchy), and the differentia which distinguish it from
other species of the same genus are stated.

Connotative, or descriptive, definition, in which a list of properties sufficient to make the phenomenon readily recognizable is set
forth.

Denotative, or illustrative, definition, in which the class to
which the object belongs is made clear by listing known objects
that belong to the same class.

Genetic definition, in which the object to be defined is made
known by describing the process through which it has become the
thing it is.

Etymological definition, in which the meaning of the term is
stated as the sum of the root meanings of the source words.

Teleological definition, in which an object is described in
terms of its ultimate purpose or use.

Operational definition, in which the object is described in terms
of its dynamics, or exact mode of functioning. (This term is sometimes used, incorrectly, to mean an arbitrary definition introduced
tentatively for the purposes of a single operation, not intended to
have general validity or acceptance).

To summarize: Definition is a process in which the comprehension of the concept, or class, is rendered more distinct by development about a dominant, essential, or generic character, and by the
subordination or even submersion of nonessential or accidental
details.

Definition is intermediate between mere *recognition* of that which is characteristic or typical and *description* or *analysis* of the whole nature of the thing, or of the class to which it is ascribed.

By definition both the generic character, or *essence,* and the *specific differences* and the *relations* are made first *logically* distinct and then explicit in language.[6]

The chief rules, or criteria, to be remembered in connection with definitions are:[7]

1. A good logical definition refers a term to its proximate genus, i.e., next higher class, and states its essential differentia.

2. A definition must give the essence of that which is to be defined. The definiens (subject) must be equivalent to the definiendum (predicate); it must be applicable to everything of which the definiendum can be predicated and applicable to nothing else.

3. A definition must state *all* the essential attributes of the object that is being defined, yet it must include *no more* and *no less* than the object or implicative system to which it relates.

4. A definition must not be circular; it must not, directly or indirectly, contain the subject to be defined. It should be expressed in other than cognate or synonymous terms.

5. A definition should be as concise, simple, and direct as possible; it should not be expressed in figurative or obscure language.

6. A definition should be in positive rather than in negative terms.

Class

Classes are the constituent elements of the classification. Confusion in the precise delineation of the separate classes will defeat the entire purpose of the classification. The best definition and criteria for *class* are to be found in Bliss (slightly modified here):[8]

A class consists of all the things that are, have been, or may be, related by likeness and differentiated by unlikeness from all other things, in the essential, significant, and selective characters, properties, and relations by which it is defined.

The extension of a class comprises all the things, real or conceptual, known or knowable, existent, past or future, that are, or may be, comprehended by its definition.

---

[6]Bliss, *op. cit.,* pp.134-35.
[7]Cohen and Nagel, *op. cit.,* p.238.
[8]*Op. cit.,* pp.132-33.

The likeness of the things classed or the differences among the classes may inhere in (1) a single significant or important character, property, or relation, (2) in any combination of these, or (3) in the whole nature, or "essence" of the thing; that is, it may be partial, relational, essential, or complete; it may be intrinsic or extrinsic; and it may be qualitative or quantitative.

The class is the totality of the things defined; it is all the things in their entirety as wholes, not merely their properties, qualities, or "essences," though it is by these that the things are likened or differentiated and the class is defined.

The class is *potentially* complete in that it comprises not only existent, but all past and future, or possible, things that may be defined by its definition and named by its name. It is not *presently* complete for it is not static. It is developmental in its extension, comprehension, and definition.

Group

Groups, in contrast to classes, are aggregates, or composites; they are selective, may comprise parts of several classes, are localized or enumerable, and temporary. They are not comprehensive, even potentially, nor are they totalities as classes are. Library displays, or quick reference collections, are normally groups rather than classes of books. Groups appear not infrequently in all practical classification systems, including bibliothecal systems, and may be quite useful for special purposes. Nevertheless, because of their fortuitous and pragmatic nature they are likely to give rise to overlappings or hiatuses in the system. When they are used at all they must be used with continual awareness of their nature.

Intension

The logical term *intension* is frequently used in several senses, which must be distinguished if confusion is to be avoided:

1. The intension of the term (object, case, or concept) may be understood as the sum total of attributes of the term *present in the mind of the person by whom the term is employed.*
2. The intension of the term may be understood as signifying the totality of attributes *essential* to it as the term it is. "Essential" is here understood to mean the necessary and sufficient condition for regarding any item as belonging within the class

designated by the term. Because this condition is usually established by conventional usage, intension in this sense is known as
conventional intension, or *connotation*--one of the acceptable modes
of definition.

3. Finally, the intension of a term may signify *all* the attributes
that the objects denoted by the term have in common, whether these
attributes are known or unknown, essential or accidental.

Another term frequently used with essentially the same meaning is "comprehension."

Extension

The *extension* of a concept or term is the whole range of concrete objects, lower classes, cases, or instances in which are found
the distinctive characteristics comprising the *comprehension,* or
intension, of the term. *Denotation* is synonymous with extension,
as *connotation* is with intension.

Classify

The verb *to classify* has two meanings:

1. To *make or conceive* a class, or classes, from a plurality of
things. It implies the likening of things to form the nucleus of a
class, and that thereafter other things so likened are referred to or
assigned to the class.

2. To *arrange* classes in some order or to relate them in some
system according to some principle or conception, purpose, or interest. It implies not only that things are classed and that classes
are formed or conceived but also that classes themselves are arranged and systematized.[9]

Classification

Berwick Sayers states that classification has four accepted
meanings:[10]

a. The intellectual process by which our mental concepts . . .
are recognized to have likeness or unity and by this likeness
or unity are set in relation to one another. This is the logical and real meaning.

---

[9]Bliss, *op. cit.,* p.143.
[10]Berwick Sayers, *op. cit.,* p.79.

   b. The act of arranging actual things ... so that they represent
      the abstract arrangement in (a). This is practical classifying.

   c. The written or printed schedule of terms which represent a
      system of classification. This is called a classification
      scheme.

   d. The act of placing things or books in their appropriate places
      in the classification scheme. This is classing.

Although the emphasis that Berwick Sayers places upon *likeness*
may be questioned, the distinctions he makes between these four
uses of the term are clearly drawn and should be kept in mind. It
is with the first of these meanings that we are concerned here.

Baldwin's *Dictionary of Philosophy* and the *Encyclopaedia Bri-
tannica* also define classification as the process of assembling like
things. Broadfield, although he has given no precise definition of
classification, rejects this emphasis upon *likeness* and insists that
difference may be of greater importance.[11] Bliss has evaded the
controversy and has given what seems to be the most useful definition:

   "A classification is a series or system of classes arranged
   in some order according to *some principle or conception, purpose, or interest, or some combination of such.* The term is
   applied to the arrangement either of the class names, or of the
   things, real or conceptual, that are so classified. The term
   classification is also by derivation and use the name for the
   classifying or arranging of classes, or things, as a process or
   method."[12]

Classification Systems (Types)

General classification includes within its limits the whole of
being. It is this general, or universal, classification that philosophers have sought, but this ideal must be rejected for practical purposes because the multiplicity of characteristics and purposes existing within the universe requires that such a system either be
oversimplified or be based upon so many different principles of
classification that it becomes unmanageable.

---

[11]*Op. cit.*, Chapter I.

[12]*Op. cit.*, p.143. For a discussion of "likeness" and "differentia" in classification see A. Broadfield, *The Philosophy of Classification* (London: Grafton,
1946), Chapters I and II.

Special classification deals with some part of the whole of being, as a science, an art, a special subject or cluster of subjects. Special classifications not only are limited in scope of materials included (extension) but also may be based upon any one, or a limited number, of the possible principles or characteristics--substance, function, origin, time-space relationships, etc. Thus there may be a plurality of equally consistent and useful classifications having the same field of extension. Only a few can be included here.

Natural classification has generally been considered to be classification based upon essential properties "inherent" in the thing itself, regularly occurring and inseparable from the object of classification. Natural and scientific classifications should conform to the "order of nature" as closely as is feasible.

Artificial classification is supposedly based upon the arbitrary selection of an accidental trait or form of behavior not physically inseparable from the objects to be classed (beings that live on land, in water, or in air, as animals, fish, and birds, for instance). To be useful, however, such a classification must be based upon a characteristic that recurs with the same certainty as though it were "inherent." The distinction between natural and artificial classification therefore is largely spurious; it derives from the belief that there is one universal, general, and eternally valid system, which can be found in "nature," once our knowledge is adequate. If that idea is rejected, and the possibility of equally valid systems of classification based upon a variety of principles is recognized, there is no need to make such a distinction. [13] Two important and common kinds of artificial classification are alphabetic series of names and arithmetical arrangements of objects according to assigned numbers.

In addition to special classifications of separate subject fields or types of phenomena, there are systems based upon relational attributes such as the spatial or the temporal.

Geometric classification arranges objects according to their position in space. Geographic and astronomic systems are the best pure examples, but every bibliothecal system has special arrangements for the subordinate classification of spatial relations. In some cases the introduction of such arrangements constitutes a violation of the primary principle of division of the system and interferes with the logical development of the schematism. [14]

Historical, or evolutionary, systems of classification arrange events according to their positions in a time series. Again, bibliothecal systems introduce chronologic subdivisions as a subordinate

---

[13]Cohen and Nagel, *op. cit.*, p.223.
[14]Piper and Ward, *op. cit.*, p.280.

principle similar to the geographic provisions. At its best, evolutionary classification consists in transforming a collection of similars into a genealogical tree, showing phases, or stages, of continuous development.[15]

Types of classification may also be identified with respect to the internal structure of the classification itself:

Hierarchical classification is the traditional and by far the most prevalent form, deriving from the philosophies of Plato and Aristotle. It may be defined as the arrangement of things (objects, concepts, etc.) into genera, species, and subspecies, according to their similarities and differences.

The concept of classification as a hierarchy was probably the first to develop; at least, that is the opinion expressed by Durkheim and Mauss in a discussion of primitive forms of classification.[16] Observation of the classifications of primitive peoples discloses that they closely reflect the social organization of the tribe. The first "classes," according to this theory, were classes of men, and the classification of physical objects was mainly an extension of previously established social classification. The hierarchy of type and subtype in logical classification, for which neither the sensory world nor the human mind offers a model, parallels the hierarchical pattern of earlier forms of social organization. Thus all objects, both animate and inanimate, in the environment were classified as belonging to this or that clan, phratry, or other kinship group.

In bibliothecal classification the tradition of the hierarchy is particularly strong. All the standard systems — Dewey, Cutter, Library of Congress, Bliss—and many that are less generally used follow such a pattern.

The main principles of hierarchical classification are:

1. A hierarchical classification proceeds by the assembly of the groups of sciences or of the principal fields of knowledge into main classes or divisions which are dictated by the theory of knowledge accepted. Such classes have great extension and small intension.

2. The process is continued by the designation of differentiating qualities within each main class, and thus subclasses or subdivisions are made.

3. Each subdivision in turn is divided by further differentiating qualities to produce still further subdivisions, and by still others

---

[15]*Ibid.*

[16]Emile Durkheim and M. Mauss, "De quelques formes primitives de classification," *Année Sociologique*, VI (1901-1902), pp.1-72.

successively to make sections and subsections, until further subdivision is impossible or impracticable.

4. Every subdivision of a class is subordinate to the class heading and the sum of these subdivisions is the whole meaning of the class term, but each single set of subdivisions may consist of classes of equal rank. These must be coordinated by likeness, or "collocated."[17]

The summation of the constituent elements of hierarchical classification finds its classic expression in the *Aristotelian predicables* —the five types of predicates that may be affirmed or denied of a subject in a logical proposition — as identified by Aristotle and later modified by Porphyry. These predicables are:

1. *Definition*. A definition, according to Aristotle, is a phrase signifying a thing's "essence." By the "essence" of a thing he understood the set of fundamental attributes which are the necessary and sufficient conditions for any concrete thing to be the thing of that type. "Essence," according to Aristotle, is that which makes a thing that which it is and not something else. Definition is the conventional intension of a term, the enumeration of its essential attributes.

2. *Genus*. The logical definition must contain two terms as its components — the genus and the differentia. A genus is identified by the "essence" common to a number of things that among themselves exhibit differences in other properties.

3. *Differentia*. The differentia is the characteristic attribute which distinguishes one species from all other species in the same genus.

4. *Property*. A property is an attribute common and peculiar to a subject, but not part of its "essence"—a predicate which, though it does not indicate the "essence" of a thing, yet belongs to that thing alone, and can be predicated convertibly of it.

5. *Accident*. An accident is a proposition not formally derivable from the definition, an attribute which may or may not be predicated of every manifestation of the subject.

From this list of five predicables Porphyry omitted *definition* from his Latin version and substituted *species,* which he defined as that portion of the genus distinguished by a given differentia.

Referential classification is a pragmatic and empirical system in which the constituent elements are related with reference to a single isolated trait, property, or use, without respect to other characteristics. Referential classification admits the possibility

---

[17]Piper and Ward, *op. cit.,* p.280.

of regrouping the same universe of things according to a different trait, property, or use. Such a classification is predicated upon the obvious truth that any single unit may be meaningful in any number of different relationships, depending upon the immediate purpose. In referential classification it is the external relations, the environment, rather than the "essence" of concepts, that are all important to the act of classifying.[18]

Relationship is not a universal, but a specific fact unique to the things related (the relata), and just as these relations reveal the nature of the relata, so the relata determine the character of the relationship. If utility is the primary objective of classification, it logically follows that the most useful classification will be one so specific to a given situation that the groupings will be determined by the relationships that are most meaningful in that situation. Such pragmatic classification denies the existence of the "essence" of the thing classified, for each single relationship depends upon a single property of the object being classified.

Example: A tree is an organism to the botanist, an esthetic entity to the landscape architect, a manifestation of divine benevolence to the theologian, a romantic retreat to a pair of lovers, a source of potential income to the lumberman. There is no "essence of the tree; the tree is really all of these things, and much more. Every separate frame of reference accentuates a part of the totality of attributes of the object with which it is dealing because only one part is relevant to a given specific purpose, and for that purpose the relevant part becomes the "essence." It is the variety of possible frames of reference including the same objects that has given rise to the need for special classification systems for special libraries.

This denial of the existence of an absolute "essence," and the assumption of relativity in classification, is repugnant to logic, which maintains that there must be for every thing a core that constitutes its individuality, without which it would not be the thing it is, and of which its other characteristics are merely properties. But concepts are the creation of human thought in pursuit of some particular enterprise or end; they are segments of human experience, which itself is never static, endowed with names and fashioned to suit human purposes. Because the tree has been analyzed into its organic constituents by the botanist, man has come to consider these organic properties as its distinguishing feature, but this concept is no more the "essence" of tree than is the romantic

---

[18]J. H. Shera, "Classification as the Basis of Bibliographic Organization," in: J. H. Shera and M. E. Egan, eds., *Bibliographic Organization* (Chicago, University of Chicago Press, 1951), pp.83-88.

symbolism by which it has been known to lovers. Both "essences" are the creation of the human mind.

Multidimensional classification may be applied to either hierarchical or referential systems. It differs from the pure form of either of these in that it makes conscious and deliberate use of multiple principles of categorization and is so constructed that any combination of these principles can be isolated for any given purpose. To add one or more dimensions to a hierarchical system based upon a single principle involves the construction of a separate hierarchy based upon the new principle and the imposition of the new pattern to all or part of the original system, thus adding a new dimension wherever required. The geographic form numbers, which may be applied wherever appropriate in the Dewey Decimal System, illustrate this procedure.

Example: Chemical compounds may be classified according to their constituent elements as one principle. The same group of compounds may be independently classified according to a physical property, such as solubility in a given list of solvents. Multidimensional classification makes it possible for these two independent schematisms to be brought into relationship at any point within either. The addition of other principles makes possible the establishment of foci of convergence, by means of which all the relationships inherent in the schematisms may be collocated.

Attempts to introduce the multidimensional principle into bibliothecal classification are exemplified in the Universal Decimal Classification, the Colon Classification developed by Ranganathan, Mortimer Taube's proposal of "coordinate indexing," and Farradane's scientific or inductive system.[19]

The purpose of classification is not only to assemble like things and to separate unlike things but also to show the relations between things. The hierarchical classification, in its pure form, is best adapted to show the extent to which an instance or object manifests the same characteristics as those in the class above or below it in

---

[19]For description and discussion, see:

S. C. Bradford, *Documentation,* 2d ed. (London: Crosby Lockwood and Son Ltd., 1953), Chapters III, XI (on U.D.C.).

S. R. Ranganathan, *Elements of Library Classification* (Poona: N. K. Publishing House, 1945).

Bernard I. Palmer and A. J. Wells, *The Fundamentals of Library Classification* (London: Allen and Unwin, 1951) (emphasis on Colon Classification).

J. H. Shera and M. E. Egan, eds., *Bibliographic Organization* (Chicago: University of Chicago Press, 1951). Papers by Mortimer Taube and S. R. Ranganathan, pp.57-71, 94-108.

J. E. L. Farradane, "A Scientific Theory of Classification and Indexing and Its Practical Applications," *Journal of Documentation,* 6, No.2 (June 1950), pp. 83-99; 8, No.2 (June 1952), pp.73-92.

the hierarchy. Relations of conjunction or of sequence, in which one instance regularly occurs with another or as a consequence of another, are difficult to show in a hierarchical system but lend themselves well to multidimensional classification. Hierarchical classifications are developed deductively, beginning with the assumption of the unity of all knowledge and *dividing* knowledge progressively by adding distinguishing characteristics to the intension of each class. Multidimensional classifications, although not all of them are free of dependence upon hierarchical precedents or principles, tend to be developed inductively by isolating definable classes at the lowest level and *combining* them according to the relationships that are important in the particular situation. The principles for inductive classification construction are still in the formative stage and no attempt will be made to treat them here. The following rules for division, however, are long established and offer helpful guides to consistency in any form of classification.

Division

Logical division is that process by which a species is differentiated from the genus, or a subspecies from its species, by adding a distinguishing characteristic to the definition of the larger class. Thus groups within the more general class are set off from one another through possession of some attribute not common to the class as a whole.

Example: The Oak is a species of the genus Tree, but it is a whole tree, not a part of a tree (such as the trunk, a branch, or a leaf) and the Oak is not adequately defined in the definition of the genus Tree. The Oak is defined through the definition of Tree *plus* the identification of those characteristics in which it *differs* from all other species of the genus Tree.

If the characteristic is the focal point of the process of division, and if the act of classification implies the discovery and identification of successive differences, four rules of division govern the process of classification.

Rules of Division:

1. The use of characteristics, whether natural or artificial, must be consistent at each stage of division, one principle of division being exhausted before another is introduced. This insistence that a division be based upon a single principle or characteristic avoids the fallacy of *cross division* or overlapping.[20]

---

[20]Berwick Sayers, *op. cit.*, p.80; Piper and Ward, *op. cit.*, p.282.

2. The process of division must be gradual, the least amount of difference possible in the class being used at each stage. This principle of classification according to minuteness of difference results in keeping things that are closely related as contiguous as the materials themselves permit.[21]

3. The divisions of a class should be mutually exclusive, or *discrete*. This principle is really a corollary of the preceding in that cross division usually results from the presence of more than one principle of division operating at the same time.[22]

4. The divisions of a class should be collectively exhaustive considering the state of existent knowledge, the sum of the constituent divisions or species to be coterminous with the class divided. If part of the division is uncharacterized, the result, in the words of Broadfield "is a classification which is inevitably exhaustive in the sense that room can be found for anything, provided it is left nondescript." This is the fallacy of *dichotomy*, the separation of a single defined class from an amorphous undefined residue.[23]

The principles implicit in these four rules of division may be summarized thus: Every step in division must be based upon a single useful principle which is applicable to all members, the resulting divisions to be as minute as is practicable for the purpose, mutually exclusive, and exhaustive.

B.   General Principles of Logical Classification

From the preceding definitions of classificatory terms and description of the processes involved, one may proceed to evolve certain principles that relate to all types of classification and that may be understood as a frame of reference in which the classification process, or any special system, may be more fully comprehended and evaluated. But only in a limited sense are they to be regarded as rules for guidance in the making of a classification.

All being, either in whole or in part, is the province of classification. That is to say, everything in the mental or physical universe that has existed, exists, or may exist, may be the subject of classification.[24]

The above statement is not to be interpreted to mean that the whole of being, mental and physical, must be included in a *single* classification system. This is the fallacy of the universal, and the

---

[21]Berwick Sayers, *op. cit.*, p.80.
[22]Piper and Ward, *op. cit.*, p.283.
[23]Piper and Ward, *op. cit.*, p.283; Broadfield, *op. cit.*, p.38.
[24]Berwick Sayers, *op. cit.*, p.79.

cause of the mixing of principles in which many systems become hopelessly entangled.

All knowledge is relative, not only in that it is never complete, but also in the sense that knowledge exists in relation to other knowledge and by those relations it is conditioned and developed.[25]

Further, knowledge is correlative to objects, or realities, and to subjects, or minds; and knowledge is of these *things-in-relation* and of the *relations* themselves.[26]

Therefore, the classes and concepts of any classification are relative both to *existential* relations and to *knowledge* relations, and they are synthetic, developmental, and adaptable.

The arrangement or order of a classification is systematic and may conform to its author's conception of a "natural" order, or it may reflect a theory of knowledge, or it may simply be the arrangement held by the author to be most serviceable to those who are to use the system. There are as many possible orders in classification as there are relationships within its subject matter, or in the possible approaches to knowledge.

Subordination and coordination are relative and complementary. Serial, branched, and crossed structures may therefore be combined and interrelated.[27]

The collocation of related classes effects maximal efficiency in practical functional classification.[28]

The permanence of any classification, or of its components, is relative to the existing state of knowledge or to the duration of utility of the system.

II. BIBLIOTHECAL CLASSIFICATION

The emphasis given above to the principles underlying philosophical classification does not imply that bibliothecal classification is identical, or that the literature of a field can be organized in the same way and upon the same principles as the cumulative abstract knowledge within the field of which the literature is the concrete, recorded expression. The prevailing assumption that the two are identical, rather than quite different aspects of a common process, has, perhaps more than any other single factor, been responsible for the failure of bibliothecal classification to achieve its fullest utility.

Each book, or graphic record of knowledge, has its own internal

---

[25]Bliss, *op. cit.*, pp.158-63.

[26]Bliss, *ibid.*, and pp.118-31.

[27]Bliss, *op. cit.*, pp.151-56, 249.

[28]*Ibid.*, pp.146, 283, 301, 408.

structure not always consistent with that of other books in the same field or even on the same topic. Bibliothecal classification not only must reconcile these different principles of internal organization among books but also must bring out the multiple relations existing between any one of them and the relevant aspects of all others, to whatever extent close analysis is practicable and useful. Only a clear grasp of fundamental principles will enable the analyst to work simultaneously upon two distinct levels, the abstract general-ized structure of knowledge and the concrete instances of particular formulations.

As a field of knowledge develops toward maturity, and the bulk, intensity, and detail of its graphic records increase, the organiza-tion of its literature reflects this increasing specificity. The scheme for its arrangement increasingly tends to approach, in ap-pearance and general outline, the organization of knowledge itself. But there is one fundamental and important difference. Only *mono-graphs* in the strictest sense of the word — i.e., writings upon a sin-gle unitary topic — can be treated as basic units in the systematic body of knowledge. Such monographic materials, then, tend to as-sume the attributes of the *thought,* or *information, unit* (see pp. 25-26) and their relation to the bibliographic structure is relative to the frame of reference. Books that attempt to synthesize any part of the total accumulation in the field, at any level, or from any partic-ular point of view, tend to cut across the classes of the formal clas-sification of the knowledge in the field. In a very real sense, each book of this kind embodies a special classification in itself, con-structed according to the purpose of the author and embodying only those parts of knowledge useful to that purpose. To attempt to clas-sify non-monographic literature, therefore, entails an attempt to construct a classification system of subordinate classification sys-tems which may select different parts from the same total of avail-able knowledge according to a variety of different patterns. It is for this reason primarily that no classification system that is in-tended as a device for the physical *location* of volumes can ever disclose all that a given collection may contain upon a given sub-ject. If, however, classification is used as a tool for the systematic *description* of the book content, and if the classification is multidi-mensional in the sense that discrete classes are provided for the entire range of each approach to the field, then the classified cata-log can bring together in one place references to every significant treatment of any topic, regardless of the physical composition or location of the book. In other words, bibliothecal classification is characterized by the limitations which inhere in the nature of the book as a physical entity. These limitations have been so generally accepted as essential to the nature of bibliothecal classification itself that they have been absorbed even into the standard definition, and are implicit in most of the commentary upon it.

Because traditional bibliothecal classification has been so universally conceived as a blueprint for the physical grouping of books themselves, it seems desirable here to summarize in some detail its nature and characteristics as a preliminary step toward possible modification through the devices offered by the classified catalog.

A. Properties of Bibliothecal Classification

The traditional bibliothecal classification is a list of terms specifically and significantly different each from the other, capable of describing the subject content (and occasionally other characteristics) of books, inclusive of all knowledge, infinitely hospitable, in an arrangement that is linear, unique, and meaningful in the same way to both the classifier and the user. When applied to books, usually (though not necessarily) through the medium of a notation, it results in the arrangement of the books on the library shelves according to the logical principles that inhere in the schematism.

Such a definition synthesizes the seven basic *properties* of traditional bibliothecal classification:

1. *Linearity*. This property derives from the physical form of the book or the catalog card, and is the result of the fact that a library is, in effect, one continuous shelf of books and a card catalog a continuous array or sequence of cards in which each individual book or card represents a point in the line. It must follow, therefore, that any classification that can be applied to such an assemblage of units must necessarily exhibit a linear sequence of its terms.

2. *Inclusiveness*. The classification must encompass within its limits the totality of knowledge within the universe of its concern, and it therefore must comprise not only every book that has been or can be written but every *use* of books, either actual or potential.

3. *Meaningfulness of Terms*. The *terms* of the classification not only must be descriptive of the content and use of books, but they also must interpret the class for which they are the verbal correlate to the classifier and to the user of the classification in the same way. Without such uniformity of meaning the objective of the classification, the organization of recorded information for effective retrieval, is defeated.

4. *Significance of Arrangement of Terms*. The *arrangement,* or structural sequence, of the terms within the schematism must convey the same meaning to both the classifier and the user; otherwise the classification loses intelligibility.

5. *Differentiation.* Though *likeness* has generally been assumed to be the basic principle of classification, the process of classifying implies the determination of successive *differences.* It therefore follows that differences between terms must have the same meaning for both classifier and user or the terms will not be discrete.

6. *Uniqueness of Arrangement of Terms.* This property derives from the significance of arrangement of terms, and is an insistence upon there being one, and only one, possible place for each subject; but it does not deny the possibility of differing points of view in the treatment of any one subject. It does decree that identical subjects observed from identical points of view and to be used for identical purposes must coalesce into one, and only one, class.

7. *Unlimited Hospitality.* A classification must provide a place for every constituent part of the universe of which it treats; it must provide for things tangible and intangible, real and imaginary, existent and nonexistent, in the past, in the present, and in the future.

B. Limitations of Bibliothecal Classification

From these properties arise four limitations that inhere in traditional bibliothecal classification.

1. *Unidimensionality.* Because a bibliothecal classification is linear, it is necessarily unidimensional. A shelf of books, or a tray of catalog cards, or a page of a printed catalog is a projection of a straight line, and any unit thereon can have *position,* with reference to those preceding and following, but not *dimension.* But the relationships among books are polydimensional.

Thus the classifier of books as physical objects is forced into the dilemma so graphically presented by William James:

"Whichever one of these aspects of its being I...class it under, makes me unjust to the other aspects. But as I am always classing it under one aspect or another, I am always unjust, always partial, always exclusive. My excuse is necessity — the necessity which my finite and practical nature lays upon me. My thinking is first and last and always for the sake of my doing, and I can only do one thing at a time... All ways of conceiving a concrete fact, if they are true ways at all, are equally true ways ... The same property which figures as the essence of a thing on one occasion becomes a very inessential feature upon another."[29]

---

[29]William James, *The Principles of Psychology* (New York: Henry Holt, 1890), vol.II, p.333.

2. *Inconsistency of Organization.* No bibliothecal classification can be made consistent throughout with respect to its principle of differentiation, and hence it cannot be a single continuous hierarchy or progression from general to specific to more specific. In practice it must be a series of more or less independent and self-sufficient orders loosely assembled into a pseudohierarchy by an overall design.

3. *Inherent Incompleteness.* This limitation is the product of the striving for infinite hospitality — the provision for all recorded knowledge, past, present, and future — which presupposes either a static universe or the ability to predict all future knowledge. Bibliothecal classification, to be practicable, must be developmental. Its infinite hospitality can be only potential, and this potentiality must be extended to provide for new dimensions or new principles to be superimposed upon, or related to the old.

4. *Complexity.* This is a relative limitation, the importance of which varies with the structure of the field and the conceptual framework in the mind of the user. Complexity is a limitation only when it leads to confusion.

C. Notation

The preceding definition of traditional bibliothecal classification included the element of notation which, though it is not an *inherent* characteristic of such classifications, is a *practical* characteristic so necessary to the effective arrangement of physical objects that it partakes of the nature of an essential attribute that distinguishes in part the classification of books (or other physical objects) from the classification of pure knowledge. It is therefore important to devote some attention to the nature and properties of notation.

A *notation* is a convenient and economical array of symbols, possessing a *unique* and *necessary* order which, when applied to the terms of the classification, results in the ordering of the elements of the schematism.

Notation serves three purposes:

1. As the agent by which the terms of the classification are transmitted to the objects to be given a logical organization under those terms.

2. As a convenient shorthand technique for expressing the terms of the classification.

3. As a key to the organization and structure of the classification schedule. Without notation, interpretation of the scheme applied would necessitate constant reference on the part of the user to the schedule itself.

There are but two basic considerations in relating the notation to the classification:

1. The notation must possess a sufficiently *broad base* (i.e., an adequate array of symbols) to accommodate the terms of the classification.

2. Notation *follows* classification. It must not be used as a mold into which the pattern of the classification is poured or forced. Failure to observe this second principle has been largely responsible for many of the weaknesses in the Dewey Decimal Classification and, by transfer, the Universal Decimal Classification. In both, the notation has frozen the structure into a rigid and inflexible pattern.

The desirable properties of a notation are *brevity, simplicity,* and *flexibility*. The last is that property of a notation that admits of adjustability or expandability in response to the intercalation of new classes or subclasses in the classification scheme without violating either the structural design of the classification or the logic inherent in the order of the notation. *Mnemonic value* is any property of a notation that facilitates memory, such as alliteration, recurrent symbols with identical meaning, recurrent schedules, series, or symbolic combinations.

A notation is said to be "pure" when it uses only one kind of symbol (numerical, alphabetic, etc.). When a notation uses more than one kind of symbol it is said to be "mixed."

D. "Enumerative" and "Synthetic" Classification

At this point it should be emphasized that there are two major types of bibliographic classification — the "enumerative" and the "synthetic." The former is the traditional form of bibliothecal classification and is customarily used as a convenient tool for the grouping of books, and similar material. Use of an enumerative classification places upon the verbal headings of the subject catalog the burden of isolating the subsections of the groups specified in the classification and the responsibility for indicating the relationships not synthesized by the classification scheme.

A classified catalog, however, demands of the classification upon which it is based that it isolate specific subjects and synthesize such subjects as does the dictionary catalog with its alphabetic subject headings, for there must be no difference between the dictionary and the classified catalog in the ability of each to isolate specific subjects. This means that the classification system must provide coextensive class numbers for specific subjects just as the dictionary catalog attempts to render them into specific subject headings. To do this the classification system must be capable of development in such a way that it is able to describe a specific subject in terms of the notation just as readily as the dictionary catalog can describe it in terms of verbal subject headings, and perhaps with even greater specificity. A synthetic classification is the only type of classification capable of meeting this requirement.

Acceptance of this principle of synthetic classification, therefore, demands of the classification used that it should provide but *one* entry for each subject; e.g., "the genetics of dogs" would appear in the classification under "dogs" or "genetics," not under both. This is, of course, a denial of the basic idea of the "uniterm" system. Because many subjects consist of more than one element, it becomes necessary to formulate a rule for the construction of class numbers that will maintain a uniform order of the elements. Such a sequence might possibly follow that of Ranganathan — personality, matter, energy, space, and time.

E. Multidimensional Classification as a Solution to the
    Philosophical Dilemma of Bibliothecal Classification

From what has been said above concerning the nature and properties of the process of bibliothecal classification, it is clear that it differs from the intellectual process of philosophical classification in a variety of fundamental ways. He who constructs a philosophical classification enjoys the freedom to fragmentize the universe of his concern in any way most appropriate to his purpose, to create those fragments in any magnitude that he may desire, and to so integrate the structure of his hypothetical schematism as to reveal any relationship he may wish to display. He is free to make these decisions because he is dealing with intellectual abstractions that are themselves constructs of the human mind. He is limited only by the extent of his knowledge, his powers of perception of relationships, and the fertility of his imagination.

However, he who seeks through bibliothecal classification to organize recorded information is much less free. First of all, he is compelled to use only that which has been written about, and the magnitude of the fragments which comprise the universe of his concern is largely made for him. Similarly, the relationships by which these fragments are associated are finite and, for him, largely predetermined. If he is not actually dealing with the arrangement of physical objects (books), he is at least compelled to arrange the physical representation of these objects (catalog cards or bibliographic entries). Such decisions as he is free to make must be shaped by his understanding of the uses to which society puts the materials he is attempting to classify.

Second, while philosophers talk about classification involving "the whole of being, either abstract or concrete," in practice philosophical or scientific classification systems undertake to organize only *knowledge*. Since the ultimate aim of every field of knowledge is to produce a body of generalizations of ever increasing generality or abstraction, the material to be organized is abstract and is limited to abstractions about only those phenomena which have been integrated into the structure of the field. Such abstractions are related to the world of reality through the phenomena to which they refer, but the phenomena themselves need not be included in all their diversity in the classification system.

Any *practical* classification, however, must include not only the fundamental knowledge or body of abstract generalizations but also the concrete and particular instances and the factors of social organization which participate in the manipulation of both abstract and concrete or particular elements. Knowledge about art, for instance, can be systematically classified as principles of aesthetics; but when one must deal with any collection *exemplifying* these principles there must be arrangements for classifying not only the knowledge about the fundamental principles but also the particular instances or examples themselves, as well as information about the social conditions of any place or time that may have influenced the character of particular instances and even the social or institutional arrangements for the marketing, preservation, or study of them.

These three elements — knowledge, the objects studied, and the agents — are essential ingredients in every practical situation, and books are likely to be written about any one of them, any part of any one of them, or any possible combination of parts of all three. This possibility explains much of the complexity and the inconsistency of bibliothecal classification. The best solution devised so far seems to be the multidimensional system, which permits separate schematisms for each necessary element with the possibility of interrelating the separate schematisms when and where desired.

For instance, the chemist sets himself the task of exploring the nature of *matter;* he therefore organizes his findings around a classification of matter, and a handbook that summarizes knowledge in this field will be effectively organized in this way. However, the writing of books will follow this pattern only to a limited extent; books will be written about *properties* which occur in several classes of matter, their *uses,* their *sources,* or about the *methods,* or *theories,* used as tools in advancing chemical knowledge. Books in this field may be organized about any one of these approaches, yet because each of these foci of organization inevitably refers back to *matter* itself, there will be many overlappings of classes if each of these separate principles of organization of the literature

is used as a basis of class division in a bibliothecal classification.
Furthermore, if to these approaches are added those of the various
groups that are concerned with *applications* of chemical knowledge
or processes, the sources of confusion will be multiplied. The
principles of the organization of knowledge derive from the character of the knowledge — the principles of organization of bibliographic
units must derive from the characteristics of the contents of these
bibliographic units. The two will correspond to a limited extent
only. It is necessary to have much more explicit information on
these points of correspondence than we now possess.

III. CHARACTERISTICS AND STRUCTURE OF THE LITERATURE

The literature of any given field may be described in terms of
the structure and content of the literature itself, without reference
to any particular kind of library or any particular type of use to
which the literature may be put. Or it may be analyzed as representing the kinds of documentation that would be required to solve
a particular problem or set of problems, to meet the needs of a
particular group of users, or to fulfill the objectives of a special
library collection. In approaching the choice or the construction
of a classification system the librarian must analyze the literature
to be organized in terms appropriate to his own situation, for the
pattern of analysis or the kinds of questions asked about the literature will vary from one situation to another. The two patterns of
analysis identified above can be discussed here only in the most
general terms, but perhaps enough can be said to indicate the
method to be employed and the direction that a more intensive
analysis must take.

A. Analysis of Literature — Content

Bacon's threefold division of literature derived from the human
faculties of memory, reason, and imagination is still valid, and the
identification of recorded information in these terms has formed
the basis of the traditional disciplines of the social sciences, the
natural sciences, and the humanities. One scarcely needs to stress
the point that the content of the literature of these three fields exhibits quite different characteristics, and its structure follows a
widely varying pattern. The primary literature of the social sciences records the particular manifestations of human behavior,
that of either individuals or groups. The primary literature of the
natural sciences consists for the most part of reports of experimentation from which may be derived basic principles or "laws"

characteristic of the entire class of events thus being scrutinized.
The primary literature of the humanities is the creative work of
the human mind.

Similarly, the secondary works deriving from the primary records will exhibit differences peculiar to each. In the social sciences the secondary works, in general, represent attempts to collect, synthesize, and interpret the particular events described in
the primary literature in such a way that conclusions or generalizations similar to those of the natural sciences may be established.
To accomplish this the literature must be augmented by a considerable body of writings that represent opinion — opinion concerning
the basic theories around which the particular events are to be clus-
tered, opinion concerning the validity of the interpretations of the
several classes of primary events, and, finally, opinion concerning
the advisability of various means of applying the findings or generalizations of the discipline to the actual conduct of social affairs.
By contrast the secondary literature of the natural sciences is far
more compact than that of the social sciences. The possibility of
controlled experimentation from which the basic principles of these
sciences are derived reduces the literature of opinion to a minimum.
The content of the secondary literature is a relatively small body of
compiled factual information, largely in the form of handbooks and
basic texts, which becomes obsolete in a relatively short time, and
because of its high degree of precision is relatively easy to organize and to use. The secondary literature of the humanities is of
necessity almost entirely opinion, is constantly augmented as each
new generation evolves its own interpretations, and very little of
it ever becomes really obsolete.

In undertaking the analysis of the literature of any subject field
one asks such questions as:

1. What are the primary data of the field? Must they be dealt
   with individually or collectively as classes? In what form
   and in what media are they recorded?

2. Can the results of study in the field be expressed in the form
   of established and generally accepted principles or facts?

3. Are the established facts readily available in compact and
   well-organized form or are they widely dispersed in a variety of publications in which they originally appeared?

4. What are the important schools of thought in the discipline,
   and what is the pattern of publication by which they are
   represented?

5. How important is specialized opinion in this field of study, and what are its foci of controversy?

6. Are expressions of public opinion as reflected in the more popular media of communication of concern in the field of study, and is it important that the results of specialized study be interpreted in the popular media?

7. How important is methodology to the development of the field, and does it require special treatment in a significant proportion of the total literature of the field?

8. Is the terminology of the field sufficiently specialized and standardized to require special treatment in glossaries, dictionaries, and encyclopedias designed for the particular purpose?

9. Is the history of the field important to its present prosecution, or is it relevant only to the general history of society?

10. Is the literature of the field sufficiently discrete to support its own system of bibliographic organization, or must access to its record be sought in the more general bibliographies, indexes, and abstracting services?

11. Is the scope of the field international or local? What are the implications of this scope for the applicability of its findings and for the sources of the relevant literature?

B. Analysis of Literature — Problems, Use, Objectives

In a sense every library is planned to achieve a more or less definite and limited set of objectives, oriented around a given set of problems more or less limited in scope, and geared to expectations of use by a clientele of a definite type. However, the range of variation in specialization or generality is broad, and the extent to which the factors of problem, use, and clientele may condition the scope of the collection and the type of bibliographic organization may be seen most clearly in the more highly specialized libraries.

The traditional subject fields are the result of attempts to isolate one factor or aspect of a total situation to study it more intensively. Academic institutions and learned societies tend to follow this pattern of isolating rather arbitrarily certain parts of the whole. For these reasons any attempt to bring together all the content relevant to a certain problem or to a set of related

problems must cut across established subject fields and bring together those parts that have some bearing upon the particular problem. While the content and structure of the traditional fields are
fairly apparent and familiar, there are no equally well-mapped
guides to the many constellations of content that may arise when
the problem approach is used. This is the reason that so many
special classification systems and subject heading lists have been
required for special library use, and it is also the reason that skill
in analyzing such situations is particularly important for the special
librarian. There are no well-constructed and tested models for
such an analytical process, although it has been carried on prag-
matically in many instances, with varying degrees of effectiveness.
The questions listed here can be no more than suggestive; they must
be extended and modified for practical use, as they are intended only
to indicate the general lines which such an inquiry should pursue.

1. What is the central problem or group of problems for which
   documentation will be required?

2. Is the scope of the problem broad or specific?

3. Can this central problem be broken down into smaller parts
   each of which is sufficiently discrete to demand separate
   consideration with respect to the literature?

4. Do all parts of the problem area fall within a single well defined subject field or discipline? If not, into what other important subject areas will it be necessary to carry the literature searching?

5. To what extent will attempts to solve the central problem
   involve original research, and to what extent may the needs
   be met through already available publications?

6. If original research must be done, from what subject field
   or fields will research workers be recruited and what part
   of the literature of their subject specialties will be required to support their contribution to solving this particular problem?

7. Is the central problem or a significant part of the problem
   cluster concerned with practical affairs such as operations,
   management, financing, government, maintenance, marketing, labor relations, produce development, etc.?

8. What is the present state of bibliographic organization in the field? Is there a substantial body of literature dealing with the particular problem complex and bringing together the related parts of several subject fields? Are there published bibliographies, indexes, abstracting services and reviews designed especially for the particular problem area or must relevant parts of services designed for several related fields be drawn upon?

9. To what extent does the information required either for managerial decisions or for research occur in such ephemeral nontrade materials as company reports, labor-management agreements, advertisement clippings, etc.?

10. To what extent is the information required unrecorded and available only through personal sources?

11. In what physical form or in what media of publication are the necessary materials usually found?

12. What levels or types of presentation, in terms of scholarly, technical, managerial, or popular treatments, occur within the literature?

IV. PATTERNS OF RECOURSE TO THE LITERATURE

A pattern of recourse to literature is a set or sequence of actions by means of which a reader progresses from an interest, however diffused or however focalized, to the particular record or group of records containing information related to his interest. It may be called a "pattern" when the repetition of the same set or sequence of activities becomes habitual and sufficiently standardized to admit of model description and analysis.

Because this "pattern" is the product of individual or group habit, it is conditioned not only by the character and structure of the literature, particularly the bibliographic services, but also by factors which are entirely fortuitous. Hence it is not necessarily efficient and may be even irrational. It is not stable, but is subject to modification either through the planned improvement of bibliographic services or through increased familiarity with the existence and use of such services. For these reasons it is not wise to assume that a study of the present use of a body of literature or a set of bibliographic devices adequately represents their potential value. Nor is it wise to plan a set of bibliographic devices based exclusively upon a study of present patterns of use, for such patterns may be the product of bad habits. It is always necessary to discriminate between patterns of recourse as they *are* and patterns as they *should be* to achieve that most effective relationship between reader and material. Nevertheless, the choice or construction of a classification system for any body of literature must be firmly rooted in a thorough understanding as to which parts of the common pattern of recourse are efficient for the purpose, which parts need to be supplanted by a more effective set of habits, and which parts may well be implemented by more extensive, more intensive, or better integrated classification.

While there have been several studies of the relative productiveness of the library catalog, subject bibliographies, and classification systems,[30] there has been only one objective study of the bibliographic devices actually used in locating titles requested in a given library.[31] In the absence of any substantial body of systematic knowledge concerning the sources of information about titles requested for use, one can only hypothesize from general observation the types of needs that contribute to the establishment of habits of recourse. Direct and well-focused observation in a particular situation will enable the librarian to expand the following suggested outline with many more precise details.

A. General Types of Habits of Recourse

1. Consistent perusal of one or more learned, professional, or trade journals to keep up with *general developments* in the field of greatest interest. Such journals are usually obtained through personal subscription or membership, and the library's concern here is very limited. The same general objective is further pursued through attendance at professional meetings, informal personal contacts, or correspondence. The library may have a peripheral responsibility here in providing directory service, either through published directories or through maintenance of a file of individuals and organizations important in the field, and in locating or posting notices and programs of meetings.

2. Occasional or systematic perusal of key journals in *marginal or related fields,* the library being expected to provide these journals and to display them in such a way as to stimulate their use. The librarian may be expected to peruse such journals and to circulate to the personnel notice of articles expected to be of interest

---

[30]For instance, Grace Osgood Kelley, *The Classification of Books*...(New York: Wilson, 1937), and Raynard C. Swank, "The Organization of Library Materials for Research in English Literature," *Library Quarterly*, 15 (1945), pp.49-74.

[31]Gordon Williams, *A Study of the Bibliographic Sources Used by Library Patrons* (unpublished thesis: University of Chicago, 1952).

or use. The form of the notification may range from circulation of
the journals themselves with articles checked for attention, mimeographed lists of titles of articles from several journals, or photographic reproductions of tables of contents, to the preparation of a
complete abstracting service.

3. Periodic recourse to *summaries of the field,* usually in the
form of recently published textbooks for advanced instruction or
surveys of recent progress. The reader usually will be aware of
such titles in his own field through reviews in the journals he re-
ceives, but the library may be expected to provide not only the volumes known but also guidance as to similar summary treatments
in marginal or related fields not usually covered by the review
sections of the key journals.

4. Occasional search for *all* the literature, all the literature
published within a certain period, or the most significant literature
pertaining to a given topic. This type of recourse is a key area in
library service, for the library is expected to be able to provide
the basic list of *all* the literature on the topic, either the reader or
the librarian making the further selection by date, significance,
point of view, etc. For this purpose both the library catalog and
the accessory bibliographic services may be called into use, and
it is here that the effective integration of the catalog with other
bibliographic services is most important. In providing a systematic display of all titles in their logical relation to a given field the
classified catalog exemplifies one of its greatest values.

5. The pinpointed search for one title or a very limited number
of titles treating of one quite *specific problem* within a general
topic. This kind of search differs from the above in degree rather
than kind, but it is likely to demand the most highly refined bibliographic service, indexing, or abstracting of great specificity. When
such problems recur frequently within an organization, the library
may be called upon to supplement the published bibliographic services with a locally prepared service designed to fit the specific
needs of the organization.

6. Search for a *specific title,* already known by author and/or
title, requiring only the use of the catalog for locating the call number or, if the book is not in the collection, the use of an appropriate
union catalog, bibliography giving location symbols, or personal inquiry, to locate the nearest available copy. This is a problem in
physical accessibility, different in kind from the subject search
which is the main function of the classified catalog.

7. Search for a *specific fact.* Here the first recourse is to
handbooks, directories, encyclopedias of the subject, compilations
of data, formulae, etc., but if the fact required is not in such
sources the entire bibliographic machinery may be brought into

play in the search for the title of a book or article likely to include the desired information. The search may extend to personal inquiry facilitated by a local file of individuals or organizations known to be interested in the field, or the resources of other libraries may be utilized. As far as the catalog is concerned this type of search raises the very difficult problem of depth, or intensity, or analysis, a problem which can be solved only by the individual librarian with full knowledge of his own situation. It is obviously impossible to maintain a catalog that will serve as guide to *all* facts, and it is impracticable to attempt to include even a small number of recurrently significant facts unless the costs of frequent search exceed the costs of intensive catalog analysis.

8. Search for *primary data*. The range of possibilities here is so very great that generalization becomes difficult, yet this is an increasingly important problem for many libraries. The most pertinent cases to be considered are those in which the library is expected to maintain files of primary data, produced within the organization, such as research reports or even handwritten worksheets, or acquired from scattered outside sources as in the case of annual reports of companies in the same industry or in the same geographic area, etc., labor-management agreements acquired from unions or from companies, arbitration awards, commercially produced surveys purchased on a service basis, and so on. This kind of material presents major problems in both acquisition and organization, for it is here that the greatest intensity of analysis is required if the material is to be useful, and there is usually no published service that covers the exact material in precisely the right way for the special requirement of the personnel working with it. When the library must organize such materials, it is customary to maintain special files separate from the general catalog but the classification system may be extended to provide for use with such collections, thus integrating these special materials with similar or related materials in the general collection.

One scarcely needs to point out that no single bibliographic instrument can be made to serve all these needs. Furthermore, the relative importance, or weight, of each will vary from situation to situation and from library to library. The librarian therefore must analyze his own situation with these general patterns in mind to determine (1) those which are most vital to his clientele, and (2) those which the classification system he selects will most adequately meet.

Within this frame of reference he must further evaluate the classification systems available to him in terms of the foci of major interest to his own clientele. He may then make an

intelligent selection from existing systems or decide to construct
his own system.[32]

Finally, no situation admits of an ideal solution; every librarian
must of necessity operate within the limitations imposed upon him
by the resources at his command. Policy decisions in the choice
of a classification system and in its application must be founded
upon those sound administrative principles that will guide him to
the most efficient use of the means at his disposal.

V. ADMINISTRATIVE CONSIDERATIONS IN CATALOG PLANNING

Once a satisfactory classification system has been chosen or
constructed, the central concern of the librarian is to implement
the system so that it becomes an effective mechanism for organizing the collection. Classification is an important tool for the librarian, but it is not self-operating. It is only the structural framework around which the library's bibliographic apparatus must be
built. The planning of this bibliographic apparatus in its entirety
must be based upon certain major administrative and managerial
considerations which can be presented here only in the most general terms.

This section must of necessity be much shorter and less fully
developed than that related to classification itself because scholars
in the search for an ideal classification have developed a body of
theoretical knowledge that far surpasses in extent the recorded
knowledge concerning the theory of library administration. The
history of classification is long, but only in recent years has the
library profession begun to consider seriously the application of
managerial principles to library operations. In dealing with the
administration of the cataloging process, then, there can be little
discussion because the body of accumulated knowledge and reliable
data is itself so inadequate. Hence, one is forced to retreat to the

---

[32]Examples of special classification systems which have been published and
are usually available in any large library are:

S. H. Glidden and Dorothy Marchus, *A Library Classification for Public
Administration Materials* (Chicago: Public Administration Service and the
American Library Association, 1942).

Harvard University. School of Business Administration. Baker Library,
A Classification of Business Literature (New York: H. W. Wilson Co., 1937).

Jeannette Murphy Lynn, *An Alternative Classification for Catholic Books . . .*,
2d ed., rev. (Washington, D. C.: Catholic University of America Press, 1954).

The Special Libraries Association maintains at its headquarters a collection of special classification systems and subject heading lists which may be
inspected there or borrowed for inspection. A mimeographed list of those
available for loan may be obtained upon request.

general statement of a few principles which, on the basis of subjective opinion, would seem to be valid. Beyond this point there is no alternative but to propose further avenues of exploration.

A. Relation of the Catalog to Other Bibliographic Tools

The library catalog does not exist in a vacuum, nor is it likely to be the sole bibliographic resource of the librarian and his staff. It therefore must be so shaped as to supplement, rather than duplicate, existing bibliographic services when those services are adequate to some definable part of the needs of the library clientele. Once the needs of the library clientele have been analyzed, as suggested on pages 55-56, a thorough scrutiny of each of the existing bibliographic services should follow. Such a study would identify those services of greatest utility to the library and would help to define the scope of the catalog as well. Many such decisions will not rest on clear-cut choices, for few bibliographic services will meet precisely the local demands placed upon them. The librarian will therefore be compelled to weigh the value of such services and their inadequacies against the cost of maintaining a catalog that can provide a more satisfactory degree of control. The best-known examples of these supplementary services are, of course, the continuing bibliographic services that relate mainly, though not always exclusively, to the periodical literature. Many of the larger research libraries also find it expedient to eliminate from the subject catalog all titles adequately analyzed by the major retrospective subject bibliographies, though here too the policy of the library must be made explicit to the clientele.

B. Relation of Personal Assistance to Catalog Planning

The extent to which the catalog can be made to be self-interpretive for the user will depend upon a variety of factors: its complexity, its magnitude, the skill displayed in its organization, the degree of specialization of the subject fields it covers, and the skill of the library clientele in the manipulation of the bibliographic apparatus of the library. But the utility of almost any catalog will be improved by the addition of effective personal assistance. The amount, quality, and cost of such assistance are all important factors in determining the policy of the library in constructing a catalog that is of greater or lesser dependence upon personal interpretation.

In many libraries this personal assistance is limited to directing the user to the appropriate tools with some elementary instruction in their use; in other libraries the actual search is performed by the library staff. A catalog that will adequately meet the needs of the first group will be quite dissimilar from that appropriate to the second. In other words, the catalog should be adjusted to the degree of sophistication of those who will be using it most.

C. Relation of Type of Material to be Analyzed to Catalog
    Planning

The traditional book, or monograph, no longer occupies the dominant place in the library collections it once enjoyed. Increasingly variant forms of "publication" — serials, periodicals, research reports, near-print materials, microfilms, charts, maps, manuscript records of all kinds — are becoming important, perhaps even the major, concerns of many types of libraries. The library's policy with respect to the analysis of such documents in the catalog must be sharply defined and clarified for the user. Such policies will be shaped by the adequacy of analysis of these materials in the supplementary bibliographic instruments, the relative importance of these materials to the local situation, the means available for their analysis in other ways (e.g., information and pamphlet files), and the relative permanence of their value to the clientele either for current operations or as historical records. Materials that today appear to have only ephemeral, albeit significant, value may tomorrow have considerable historical importance, but the pattern of their organization may be quite different. It is the librarian's responsibility to determine potential significance and to make adequate provision for such a transition when the historical development of the field is an important element in the library situation.

D. Relation of the Classification System to the Shelf
    Arrangement

Traditionally, in those United States libraries having classified catalogs, the classification system used for the organization of the catalog and that for the organization of the books on the shelves has been the same, though the degree of specificity or minuteness may be somewhat greater in the former. There is no necessary relationship here, particularly where the stacks are inaccessible to the public, but in "open access" libraries, where the clientele has free recourse of the shelves, the use of a single system is probably less confusing. Policy here may be influenced by the extent to which the librarian, his staff, and the clientele regard and use the classification applicable to the books as a key to subject access to their contents. But for those who habitually use the book classification as merely a locational device there need be no coincidence between the two systems, and, in fact, the duplication of the shelf arrangement by the classified catalog may result in little more than wasted effort.

E. Control over Costs

The importance of costs in the determination of policy has been suggested throughout the preceding discussion. There are few reliable studies of the costs of cataloging and no studies of the comparative cost of maintaining a classified catalog as opposed to some other form of organization. Neither has there been any adequate study of the savings that a "good" catalog can effect in reducing other library costs or in improving the efficiency of the clientele it serves. Yet the character of the cataloging operation would seem to admit of fairly precise cost analysis in the extent to which it can be broken down into its constituent elements and each isolated for independent measurement. The savings which any given type of catalog can effect in any specified situation are perhaps less amenable to precise measurement, but at least some insight could be gained through the analysis of synthetic and precisely controlled laboratory situations. The individual librarian would be well advised to maintain accurate cost records that would supply the data for periodic management studies. Full advantage should be taken of the techniques of sampling, for the maintenance of cost accounts can itself become an unjustifiably heavy drain upon the resources of the institution.

Chapter 3

The construction and maintenance of the classified catalog system

III. Code for the Construction and Maintenance of a Classified Catalog (Detailed outline immediately preceding the section on p. 87)ı

Once the major decisions growing out of the theoretical considerations discussed in Chapter 2 have been made, the librarian is faced with the necessity of taking the several practical steps necessary to translate these decisions into an effective operating system. "System" here means not only the catalog itself, with its cluster of auxiliary files, but also the set of rules or principles relating to consistent practice in classing materials. This chapter, therefore, will be devoted to these two major topics, the set of files making up the complete catalog and a set of rules for the organization of materials within the catalog.

I. THE CATALOG AND ITS AUXILIARY FILES

The number and kind of files considered to be necessary parts of the catalog may vary from one library to another, but in general they may be listed as follows:

For Public Use

1. The classified catalog

2. Subject index, the verbal key to the class symbols used in the catalog.
   Note: An alternative to a subject index as a separate unit of the classified catalog apparatus is the filing of the index cards into the author-title catalog. This has two important disadvantages: it precludes the possibility of locating the index in filing cases immediately adjacent to the classified catalog, and it adds unnecessarily to the complexity of the author-title catalog.

3. Author and title catalog, an alphabetic guide to materials which are arranged by subject in the classified catalog.

4. Alphabetic list of periodicals received, and other aids to the use of the catalog.

For Administrative Control

5. Classification schedule, including notation.

6. Numerically arranged index of classes used in the catalog.

7. Decisions file.

8. Manual of practice.

9. Indexes to special collections of materials not included in the classified catalog.

10. Subject heading lists.

This list divides into two groups, the first four elements being intrinsic parts of the catalog system itself and the last group being auxiliary administrative aids necessary to maintain consistency and clarity within the catalog.

To these might be added the shelf list. Although it is superficially related to the catalog it is really a completely separate mechanism. The shelf list in any library, regardless of its system of classification, is traditionally regarded as a file of entries which recapitulates the arrangement of the physical units comprising the library collection as they stand on the library shelves or in other storage equipment. In actual practice, however, certain segments of the book stock (e.g., rare books, oversize volumes, miniature volumes, reference collections, reserved-book collections and the like) are customarily withdrawn from their logical positions in the classification sequence and separately housed. Thus the shelf list becomes merely an inventory of the physical units comprising the total holdings of the library, arranged in one continuous sequence according to the classification system used, or in an arbitrary shelf order when classification is not used for shelving. The shelf list may be made to assume a variety of administrative functions but its basic purpose is but twofold: (1) to facilitate the intercalation of new materials into the existing collection, in which capacity it serves not only as a check against the duplication of the same call number for two different titles but also as a supplement to the classification schedule and (2) to present an official inventory of the holdings of the library. This last is not to be confused with its assumed purpose as an instrument for the taking of an inventory, a function for which it is relatively ill adapted since it does not actually recapitulate the sequence of the physical books as they stand on the library shelves.

It has been customary in this country to use the same classification scheme for the arrangement of the books on the shelf and the cards in the classified catalog. This practice probably arose

THE CLASSIFIED CATALOG SYSTEM

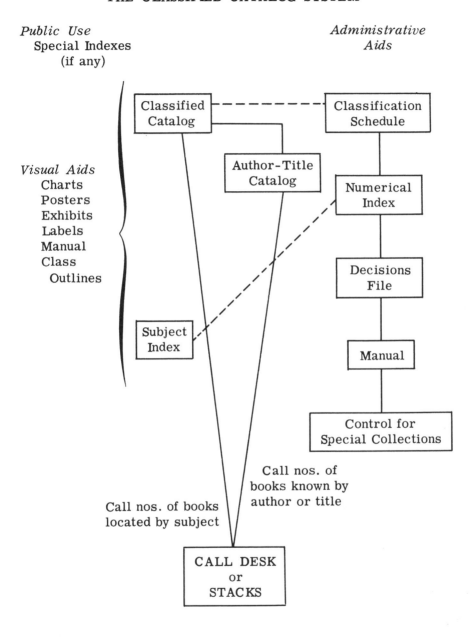

Public Use
  Special Indexes
    (if any)

Administrative Aids

Classified Catalog

Classification Schedule

Visual Aids
  Charts
  Posters
  Exhibits
  Labels
  Manual
  Class
    Outlines

Author-Title Catalog

Numerical Index

Decisions File

Subject Index

Manual

Control for Special Collections

Call nos. of books located by subject

Call nos. of books known by author or title

CALL DESK
or
STACKS

Shera and Egan   The Classified Catalog

from the fact that the classified catalog derived from the classification of the physical books, and the classified catalog was often regarded as an expanded shelf list. This identity is, however, not essential to the operation of either. Inasmuch as the classified catalog and the physical arrangement of the books serve quite different ends the schematic sequence of the one may bear no relation to the other. The classified catalog is basically a subject key to the resources of the library, the shelf arrangement is but an instrument of physical accessibility. The only requisite is that the two be so integrated that the transition from one to the other may be accomplished with a minimum of effort and a maximum of accuracy. This means no more than that each catalog card must carry the location symbol of the bibliographic unit for which it stands.

The essential parts of the catalog system, as we have seen above, are the classified catalog, the author-title catalog, the subject index, the classification schedules, and any special indexes to periodical holdings or to collections not included in the general catalog. This catalog system is graphically presented on page 67.

A. The Classified Catalog

Form

The classified catalog, like any other, may be in book form, on cards, or in any other convenient format. Because card catalogs are so much more prevalent than any other type, the use of cards is assumed throughout this discussion. If another form is to be used, only minor adjustments will be necessary. If machine manipulation is adapted to library use, major readjustments in the management of the catalog may become necessary.

Arrangement

Decisions as to arrangement must be made at two levels: the arrangement of the classes themselves and the arrangement of entries within the class.

1. *Arrangement of Classes.* The sequence of the classes is almost inevitably dictated by the notation, which has been defined as possessing "a unique and necessary order which, when applied to the terms of the classification, results in the ordering of the elements of the schematism" (*supra,* Chapter 2, p. 48). All commonly used bibliothecal systems rely upon letters of the alphabet, numerals, or a combination of both, for their notation, and the arbitrary order implicit in the symbols chosen must be followed.

It is the decimal principle that makes possible the intercalation of new terms into the classification without violating the logical order of the schematism, and this principle should be observed whether or not decimals appear in the notation. Adherence to this rule makes possible the arrangement of the classes in the arbitrary order prescribed by the notation with complete confidence that the materials themselves will appear in the logical order of the original classification.

2. *Arrangement of Entries Within Classes*. Inasmuch as the arrangement of the entries within the class is not governed by the notation, a wider choice of arrangement is possible and the same degree of consistency is not required. The usual arrangement is alphabetically by author (or title when used in lieu of author) but other frequently used arrangements are: chronologically by date of publication (or date of text) with latest date first if emphasis is on recent publications; geographically by country, state or other political or geographic unit; by language (either of original text or of translation); by literary form; or by any combination of the above, i.e., geographic further divided by period, etc. Different sections of the classification may suggest different principles of arrangement; the only requirement here is that the principle chosen be applied consistently throughout the entire class or subclass to which it is applied. A decision made with respect to any class should be recorded, with some indication of the reasons, for the benefit of future classifiers.

Entry

In preparing the cards for the catalog, the form of entry, or bibliographic form, will vary from full bibliographic information, in those libraries in which the unit card system is used, to simplified cataloging, where only author, short title, and imprint are used on all cards other than the main entry card (normally the author entry). The minimum information needed will vary from one library to another according to the clientele and also from one type of material to another within each library. Decisions relating to each type of material should be recorded in the decisions file to ensure consistency of treatment.

Two alternatives may be considered for indicating on the cards the location or locations which each catalog entry is to be given in the classified catalog: (1) adding the class number (filing location) at the top of each entry, or (2) indicating the filing class number at the lower margin of each entry. The first can be used with either the separately typed short-form cards or the printed unit card

system. In the second, the guide card must be depended upon as
the readers' access to the catalog, and a guide card for every
class number used in the classified catalog is required (see p. 71).

Whatever practice is followed, every class number to be used
must be recorded on the main entry card as in any tracing. If the
main entry card is used as copy for the unit card the tracings will,
of course, appear on each card. In order to avoid confusion, the
appearance of the card should conform as closely as practicable to
the American Library Association standards for author and title
entry, the main difference being that the class number replaces
the verbal subject headings of the traditional dictionary catalog (cf.
Library of Congress *Rules for Descriptive Cataloging*). A good
sample form for the entry to be used in the classified catalog is
given below; variations from this form should be adopted only after
careful consideration of the local circumstances which seem to
provide good reasons for modifications.

SAMPLE FORM FOR CLASSIFIED CATALOG ENTRY

```
                                      (Class Number) optional
    (Call
     No.)   (Author)_____
                (Title ...
            _____) . (Imprint ...
                              ) .
                (Collation)_____

                (Tracing ... Added entries ...
            class symbols                    ) .
```

Note: The "call no." and "class number" at the top of the card are
reversed in position in the Crerar Library catalog. The example
here is given because of the widespread use of the upper left position for the call number on catalog cards.

Guide Cards

No generally accepted basic principles for the use of guide cards, nor for the appropriate numerical ratio between guide cards and entry cards, have ever been formulated. In the classified catalog, as distinct from the alphabetic catalog, the guide card is especially important in that it not only facilitates the physical manipulation of the entries, but also reveals to the user the basic pattern of the classification. Since the utility of the classified catalog is dependent upon the extent to which it reveals the logical relationships that inhere in the literature of the subject fields represented, false economies or carelessness in the distribution of appropriate guides will seriously impair their utility as indicators of those very relationships which they are supposed to emphasize.

Although guide cards at one-inch intervals may be appropriate in a dictionary or author-title catalog, this ratio does not necessarily hold for a classified catalog. The ideal is to provide a guide card for each unique classification symbol and if the policy of omitting classification symbols from the individual cards is adopted, this practice becomes mandatory. Where subdivisions are minute and the individual subject cards few, guide cards may interfere with use. In such cases, the alternative of a single guide to cover several successive subdivisions may serve temporarily until the accumulation of material warrants separation. But whatever policy is adopted, there should certainly be a visible relation between the guides and the level of subordination in the classification. In those classes where the concentration of cards is extremely great, further subordination may be effected by the use of subordinate alphabetic or date cards, depending upon the principle of arrangement of the titles within the class.

Guide cards should reveal more than the simple notation of the classes for which they stand. In addition to the class number or symbol, each card should bear sufficient explanatory text to interpret the scope of the class. Such text may vary in length from a single word or phrase denoting the name or title of the class to a more lengthy, but concise, definition or scope note. The space limitations dictated by the physical form of the card place a premium on brevity, which, in turn, accentuates the importance of clarity and precision.

In addition to the definition that normally appears on the guide card, other information valuable to the user may also be placed there but should never be permitted to crowd or to supplant the definition. It is preferable to carry such information to one or more supplementary cards.

Classing of Materials

The mechanical, or physical, features of the classified catalog have been discussed at some length above, but the most important key to the success of the catalog lies in the rationality and consistency of the analysis of the materials. Assuming that the classification has been wisely chosen or constructed according to the principles enunciated in Chapter 2, there remains the necessity for the elaboration of a code of practice which will standardize the procedures among the many classifiers or catalogers who in the course of time will contribute to the evolution of the catalog. Although this code of practice is an intrinsic part of the classified catalog system its importance and necessary length seem to require separate treatment and it is accordingly outlined in full in a separate, section III, pages 87-103.

B. The Subject Index

The subject index is the key to the classified catalog, without which it cannot operate effectively. It is the point of entry through which the user gains access to the materials represented in the catalog; and it performs for the catalog the same function that the relative index serves for the Dewey Decimal Classification.

The subject index is an alphabetically arranged list of terms and their synonyms, descriptive of the contents of the materials classified in the catalog, together with the code symbols of the classes which represent them. It is limited to only those terms represented by the contents of the catalog, omitting classes which may appear in the classification but are not represented in the collection.

The subject index to the classified catalog, by directing the user to relevant material, serves the same purpose as the "see" and "see also" cards in the dictionary catalog. The several forms of access through the subject index may be described as follows:

Direct Entry

The simplest case, and probably the most frequent, is that in which the term employed in the catalog is identical with that which occurs naturally to the user, and all the material he may want is encompassed within the single class. *Example:*

DOORS   721.81 (Architecture)

In using the dictionary catalog the inquirer would find directly under DOORS a number of references, while in using the classified catalog he would first consult the subject index to get the number "721.81" and would then go to that number in the classified catalog to find the references. An extra step is certainly involved here, but there is also an added value in that he may find additional material in the adjacent classes "721.8," "721.811," or "721.82."

Alternative Entry

In many cases, however, the term most familiar to the user is not that employed by the classification. The dictionary catalog then makes use of the "see" reference to guide the reader to the proper place in the catalog. The subject index to the classified catalog, by contrast, eliminates this step by repeating under each synonym or alternative term the code symbol of the appropriate class. This can be done because the repetition of the code symbol in the subject index under all the terms considered worthy of inclusion requires no more cards than the listing of the terms themselves, whereas to repeat in the dictionary catalog all the references to books under all alternative terms would soon glut the catalog. *Examples:*

HEALTH RESORTS	613.12 (Hygiene) 725.75 (Architecture)

RESORTS	613.12 (Hygiene) 725.75 (Architecture)

SPAS	613.12 (Hygiene) 725.75 (Architecture)

Entry to Related Materials

Although one of the great values of the classified catalog is that it does bring together logically related materials, yet the body of our present knowledge is so vast and so complex and the interrelationships of its parts show such varied ramifications, depending upon the circumstances of practical use as well as abstract logic, that no classification can bring together all materials for all purposes. There will inevitably be related materials scattered throughout different and sometimes widely separated classes. In the dictionary catalog these scattered materials are made available through the use of "see also" references, which may send the inquirer to half a dozen different places in the catalog to collect his bibliography on a given topic. In the classified catalog neither "see" nor "see also" references are required, for the subject index entry includes both the symbol and the class heading for all classes in which related materials may appear. These references serve the same purpose as the "see also" card in the dictionary catalog, while the classified catalog has the additional advantage of making apparent those related materials that are entered in the classes preceding or following the primary class. *Example:*

DYES

> 547.18 (Organic chemistry. Cyanogen and its
> compounds)
> 547.86 (Organic chemistry. Nitroderivatives)
> 667.25-.27 (Chemical Technology. Dyeing)

By inspecting the explanatory phrase which follows the class number the user is able to identify the aspect of the subject in which he is interested. Additional subject index cards are also filed in their alphabetic places. *Examples:*

CYANOGEN COMPOUNDS

> 546.26 (Inorganic chemistry)
> 547.18 (Organic chemistry)

NITRODERIVATIVES

547.86 (Organic chemistry)
667.27 (Chemical Technology. Dyeing)

Sometimes materials are so closely related that they always
occur together or, when they occur together, they achieve a unity
that precludes discussion of one without the other. In such instances
compound, or composite, headings are used. *Example:*

TYPE AND TYPE-SETTING   655.2 (Printing and
                                        publishing)

An alternative to multiple references on each index card is the
recording of each reference on a separate card. This results in
one of two disadvantages: it greatly increases the number of index
cards for subjects referred to from several synonyms, or it requires cross references in the subject index contrary to the principle of direct approach.

Terminology of Index Entries

Choice of terms, as between scientific and popular for example,
will depend upon the nature of the library and its clientele. Whether
the policy of the library is to use scientific or popular terminology
or not, the desirability of choosing at either level that term most
frequently used or most familiar to the clientele should be emphasized. In many cases, perhaps in most libraries, both may be very
desirable. The specialist will use a specialized vocabulary in his
own specialization, but as he approaches less familiar areas his
vocabulary approaches that of the layman. Inasmuch as alternative
terms may be used rather freely in the subject index to the classified catalog, decisions reflect not so much need to choose *one* term
in preference to all others but rather the possibility of referring to
a number of terms that would naturally occur to a given clientele.

Physical Form

Throughout this discussion the assumption has been that the subject index will be in card form. The book form, although it is less flexible, does have one advantage in the possibility of duplication and distribution of copies. It is possible, although expensive, to maintain a public card index and at the same time prepare periodic editions in book or pamphlet form of all or part of the index for distribution within or without the library. New duplicating processes are less costly than letterpress, but few libraries will find the expense justifiable.

It is probably unnecessary to point out that exceptionally sturdy card stock should be used, because the subject index will be heavily used and the entries are intended to be permanent. Guide cards at frequent intervals (ratio of one to one inch, usually) to facilitate the manipulation of the file are just as necessary in the subject index as in the full catalog. These guide cards need carry no information other than the heading since they serve merely to break the file and indicate at what part of the alphabet the break occurs.

C. Indexes to Special Collections

Ideally the subject catalog should be a complete guide to the entire collection of any given library, but there are, inevitably, certain bodies of material which cannot practicably be analyzed with the desired intensity in the general catalog. Hence every library will have a certain number of locally prepared indexes to certain types of material. Examples of such indexes might be: a local history index to the local newspaper, an index of great specificity to the research reports of the parent organization, a detailed index to a file of labor agreements according to the specific provisions of the agreements (or any materials used as primary data), or a special index to a file of materials of interest as examples of a technique regardless of substantive content, e.g., propaganda, typographic styles, etc.

The utility of such indexes is greatly increased when their existence is indicated at the appropriate points in both the classified catalog and the subject index to it. They then become an integral part, or extension, of the catalog system.

Such special indexes should, of course, be kept to a minimum since they materially increase both the costs and the complexity of the system.

D. The Author-Title Catalog

The author-title catalog, which is really an independent

bibliographic instrument with its own rationale and functions, is related to the classified catalog so closely that neither can be developed without reference to the other. Each represents an entirely different organization of the library's bibliographic resources, and each has its own purposes and principles of construction.

The author-title catalog serves the same purposes as its counterpart in the dictionary catalog. It is, as its name implies, a formal record of the holdings of the library, arranged alphabetically by name of author, joint author, editor, illustrator, compiler, translator, etc., and by title of work when such titles are: (1) sufficiently distinctive to aid in identification, and (2) the sole means for the precise identification of the work.

Because of its principles of organization it cannot be interfiled with the classified catalog. The rules for its construction have already been codified by the American Library Association *(A.L.A. Rules for Author and Title Entry...)* and by the Library of Congress *(Rules for Descriptive Cataloging in the Library of Congress)*. The form of author entry used in the author-title catalog should establish the pattern of the unit card to be used in the classified catalog.

E. Other Aids to the Use of the Catalog

The utility of most library catalogs would be substantially improved by the ingenious and imaginative use of effective display materials that interpret the intricacies of this complex bibliographic instrument to the user. In this the classified catalog is no exception; in fact, because users are relatively unfamiliar with its structure, these aids are especially important to its fullest utilization. Such aids are of three basic types: (1) conspicuous labelling that will clearly indicate to the patron the several parts of the catalog system and minimize confusion as to which is the classified catalog itself, the subject index, or the author-title catalog; (2) effective displays that will set forth in simple, concise language the organization of the system and the necessary or suggested procedures for its consultation, including, perhaps, the outline of the classification system itself; and (3) elementary manuals or handbooks that will give in greater detail than is possible through the displays essential information on the design and use of the system.

No precise rules can be formulated to guide the librarian in the preparation of these aids. Neatness in their preparation is assumed, and the more "professional" their appearance the more effective they are likely to be. The need for and the variety of such aids will vary from situation to situation, and local resources in materials and imagination are the only limiting factors. Such aids may vary from the simplest of conspicuous signs or posters to elaborate charts, schematic diagrams, and even three-dimensional exhibits.

The parts of the catalog system discussed above relate to those elements that are of primary concern to the user; there remain certain administrative tools which, though they are not used directly by the public, are important to the staff, contribute to the general effectiveness of the system, and indirectly, at least, influence the patron's reaction to the system as a bibliographic service. The most important of these tools are:

The classification schedule, with notation

The decisions file

The numerically arranged index of classes used in the catalog

The manual of practice

F. The Classification Schedule

Consideration of the classification schedule is here limited to its format; the general principles of classification are set forth in Chapter 2, and the code of rules for its use will be discussed in Section III of this chapter. Any classification schedule must be supplemented by an adequate index and provided with the necessary means for constant revision. Most of the standard bibliographic classifications are equipped with indexes of some kind. Where local classifications are employed, indexing becomes the responsibility of the library staff. Such an index must necessarily recapitulate the subject index to the classified catalog, but in addition would include those categories of the classification for which no materials are present in the library collections.

In Chapter 2 one of the desirable properties of a classification was identified as "infinite hospitality." Administratively this necessitates provision for the introduction of new terms in their appropriate position in the sequence. Physically this may be accomplished either through the use of a card system or, if the schedules are recorded in book form, through sufficient interleaving for the maintenance of such a record. The latter would seem to be preferred, since in all except the smallest libraries extensive duplication of the schedules is virtually mandatory.

Revision, of course, implies much more than the mere introduction of new categories or terms. To be kept strictly current a classification schedule must be under constant scrutiny for the elimination of obsolete elements, the fragmentation of existing categories into more meaningful subdivisions, and the reassembly of related components into more useful groupings. This process of revision, as it applies to the entire classified catalog system will be considered in Section III of this chapter but attention is directed toward it here as one of the important administrative responsibilities.

G. The Numerical Index

In the numerical index are recorded for each class number all verbal headings in the subject index that refer to that class number. It is in effect the alphabetic subject index in reverse, and ensures that any alteration in any one class number will be traced through every appearance of that class number wherever it may appear in the subject index. At first thought it might appear that the classification schedule itself would perform this function, but the schedule gives for each class number only the formal caption of the class for which it stands; it does not give all possible synonyms, variants, compounds, or references within related fields. *Example:*

NATURAL DYES

    581.64 (Economic botany)
    667.27 (Natural dyes)

Under this same class number in the numerical index, in alphabetic order, will be filed similar cards for:

667.27 COCHINEAL
      DYE PLANTS
      INDIAN YELLOW (DYESTUFF)
      ISATIS TINCTORIA
      PASTEL (DYESTUFF)
      WOAD

each card giving the appropriate class numbers and explanatory phrases. The latter method makes possible additional tracing of subject index entries without withdrawing the original. It is an aid to the classifiers, since class numbers for various aspects of each subject are readily visible. These cards are duplicates of those filed in the subject index, filed by number rather than alphabetically.

H. The Decisions File

The decisions file is, as its name implies, merely an

administrative device to provide for the maintenance of consistency
in practice throughout the system. It serves the cataloger and classifier as the manual of style serves the editor or publisher. It may
treat of any aspect of the system in which ambiguity or departure
from standardized practice may occur. Since it must be so closely
integrated with local practice, it is difficult to establish general
principles to guide its evolution, except to state that it should exhibit some basic plan of organization so that related practices and
processes may be kept together. If the card form is not used, a
loose-leaf format would seem to be indicated. All recorded decisions should, wherever possible, be supplemented by concise statements of the reasons for their adoption, for without these future
generations of workers could scarcely be expected to interpret
them intelligently or revise them effectively. Finally, the decisions
file should be kept to a minimum. Constant vigilance is required
to keep it under control, but an undisciplined decisions file can
easily ensnarl its creators in the meshes of its own intricacy.

I. The Manual of Practice

The manual of practice is in effect that part of the staff manual
which relates to the work itself rather than to the conditions of
work. As in the case of the decisions file, it is closely related to
the local situation, but it might well include such elements as a description of specific operations, a flow chart of the work load,
statements of the division of authority and responsibility for specific operations, and generalizations concerning the principles
upon which the local system is constructed and expected to operate.
It interprets for the local situation the principles set forth in the
general code of practice presented in Section III. Because it is
less detailed than the decisions file it is more nearly permanent
and less subject to revision. It is a local bridge between the general code and the specific decisions file, over which general principles are brought to bear upon local problems, and local decisions
which have been adopted, tested, and approved may be assimilated
into the local code. As such, it is an effective check against unre-
stricted departure from standard practice.

II. METHODS OF ANALYSIS

The classification of books for a classified catalog is the process of assigning to each book or separate bibliographic unit the
code symbols designating those terms or classes which most precisely describe the content or other characteristics. Thus, when
the catalog has been filed in the order of the notation, the cards

describing the different aspects of the book are grouped with other cards representing like characteristics of other books.

A. Primary Classification

Primary classification is that classification in which first consideration is given to the subject content of the book as a whole, and in general it may be said to be the choice of that category in which the book would be placed physically in a shelf arrangement. This primary classification should be determined first as a point of reference, regardless of any more immediately obvious possibilities and regardless of whether or not the books are actually to be shelved according to the classification system.

The primary classification should ordinarily be chosen according to subject content of the book as a whole; this is especially important in libraries where books are arranged on open shelves according to the primary class numbers. In special situations alternative characteristics may be desirable in determining the choice of primary classification. Some of these characteristics, suitable in special collections, may be date, binding, language, literary form, publisher, class of reader for whom the book is intended, etc. Any characteristic that is of primary importance in the special library may be used, but care must be taken to ensure consistency; every book in the collection that shares the characteristic must be given the primary classification of that characteristic, regardless of its other aspects. It should be obvious that one should never class a book by the title alone, for the title may not be an accurate indication of the content. If the title is not adequately indicative of the content, the classifier should consult the table of contents, the preface, the text itself, and sometimes book reviews, handbooks, bibliographies or encyclopedias that describe the scope and interrelations of the subject in question.

Even though neither the title nor the manifest content of the text seems to reflect the exact intent of the author, such intent should be given primacy in the classification of the book. For example, a book ostensibly dealing with the foreign trade of a given country at a given period may be really an extended argument for or against a tariff, with the historical material used only as evidence for the author's argument. Such a book might be classed under the number for Tariff, with secondary entries for other aspects.

B. Secondary Classification

Secondary classification is the choice of the additional class terms necessary to describe fully and precisely other aspects of the subject content, other characteristics of the book, or important *parts* of the book (analytics). The order of consideration of these added entries may well be:

1. Added subject entries
2. Place
3. Time
4. Language
5. Form, etc.

The user of the catalog will be unaware of any distinction between primary and secondary classification, for the form of the card is no different. Nevertheless, some standardization of procedure is desirable to ensure that the classifier does not overlook any of the aspects that should be brought out in the catalog. The determination of the primary classification as a first step is useful to the classifier as a point of reference, or a "bench mark," to which all possible secondary classifications may be related. Primary classification is, of course, necessary in all libraries and for all materials, whereas the number and kind of secondary class numbers used will vary from one library to another and from one kind of material to another within a given library.

C. "Intension," or Intensity of Classification

The "intension of a term" has been defined (Chapter 2, p. 34) as the signification of *all* the attributes that the objects in the denotation (or extension) of the term have in common. In using classification for the systematic description of the content of bibliographic units, "intension" (or intensity) of classification must be adjusted to the choice of those attributes of sufficient potential utility to the clientele of the particular library to justify entries in the classified catalog.

In common library practice, this concept of "intensity" is recognized in the principles of "close classification" in the act of classing, and of "specific entry" in the choice of subject headings. When the classification system is used for the logical grouping of the physical books, close classification is the obvious application of this concept, but when the classification is used as a device for the systematic analysis and description of content in the classified catalog, further application becomes not only possible but necessary. Here, the added entries for secondary classifications assume the function of the added subject headings in the dictionary catalog to which the rule of "specific entry" refers. Some of the same criteria used in the choice or construction of the specific subject headings will apply to the choice of classes for added secondary entries In every library there are some materials that require no more than the single primary classification, but it is assumed that libraries maintaining classified catalogs do so because their functions are so specialized as to necessitate intensive analysis of a considerable part of their collections.

Thus, Merrill's rule for close classification states: "Class a book by the most specific topic that will express the character of the book." In constructing a classified catalog this rule might be expanded as follows:

1. In choosing the primary class number, use the most specific class that will express the character of the book as a whole.

2. In choosing secondary classes, use for *each* attribute which has been selected for inclusion in the analysis the most specific class that will express the character of *that* attribute.

For example, suppose a book dealing with the statistical measurement of the cost function in a group of selected industries is to be analyzed for a classified catalog. Obviously, the character of the book as a whole according to the intent of the author can best be described as a contribution to statistical methodology, the application to a series of empirical situations being intended merely to demonstrate the method. The primary classification would then be the most specific class under Statistics—Methods that will fit the method or methods developed in the book. The demonstrations of applicability to certain industries, however, may have considerable value to those interested in any one of the industries; secondary classes should be assigned to the most specific class under each industry related to the kind of information included in this book, e.g., the class number assigned to Steel Industry—Production—Cost Analysis. In a multi-axial system (such as the Colon Classification or Universal Decimal Classification) it would be necessary merely to add to the original code symbol the code symbols representing the industries involved.

Although it is possible to multiply almost indefinitely specific rules for classing particular types of materials and although such rules are helpful in maintaining consistency in a given catalog, the heart of successful classification will always be the systematic intellectual analysis. To develop a consistent pattern of intellectual analysis usually requires years of experience. It should be possible to combine the fundamentals of logic with the practical observations of skilled classifiers in such a way as to formulate a training program which would speed and facilitate the program. Appendix A, Method for the Systematic Analysis of the Materials to be classed, offers one tentative approach to such a formulation.

D. The Category of Form

Form, as it is understood in library practice, is of two types:
(1) the physical characteristics of the book as a three-dimensional
object, e.g., miniature books, and (2) the arrangement or manner
of treatment of the substantive content, e.g., encyclopedias. Examples of these types are presented in the following table:

Physical Form	*Treatment of Content*
Newspapers	Dictionaries
Periodicals and serials	Encyclopedias
Pamphlets and papers	Year-books
Reprints	Manuals and handbooks
Miniature books	Gazetteers
Oversized books	Atlases
Binding types	Directories
Films	Bibliographies
Microduplicates	Indexes
Recordings	Abstracting services
Pictures and clippings	Calendars of documents
Maps	Textbooks
Manuscripts	Dissertations
Archival material	Illustrated editions
Embossed books (Braille)	Translations
	Literary forms
	Poetry
	Essays
	Drama
	Novel
	Collected works
	Anthologies
	Festschriften
	Addresses, sermons, etc.
	Sets and series
	Musical forms
	Operas
	Symphonies
	Sonatas
	etc.

A type of record that is frequently treated as form yet does not
come within either definition above, is the government document.
Documents may display any physical form or assume any manner

of content treatment. Many libraries have elected to segregate
them because of the convenience such segregation affords in the
use of the special bibliographies and guides to their use provided
by the issuing agency. This is segregation by *source* rather than
by *form*. Nevertheless, there will be documents of such importance
to any library that entries in the catalog under the appropriate subject numbers must be made; such entries may give the documents
number as the location symbol. When documents are segregated
from the rest of the collection, conspicuous reminders that such
resources exist must be provided, perhaps among the visual aids
or charts recommended previously (p.77), among the references
on selected subject index cards, or on the information cards in the
classified catalog.

If documents are classified with the rest of the collection, prefer
subject, but classify general and miscellaneous publications with
the administrative unit represented.

The same general principles apply to international, foreign,
state and local documents, except that in cases where the issuing
governmental body does not provide for the autonomous bibliographic organization of its documents, the library will have to decide whether to integrate them completely with its general collection or whether to treat them as archival material, arranged and
classed according to the issuing agency.

Another type of material that may require special decisions concerning analysis in the subject catalog is the research report, either
produced within the organization itself or acquired from outside
sources but subject to certain restrictions as to use. Such reports
may present problems of physical form if worksheets or progress
reports, as well as the final statement of results, must be incorporated. The customary practice in handling such materials is to arrange them by project number, which then becomes the location
symbol but does not interfere with the classification of the content.
The problem of restricted use (security classification) may necessitate segregation of the materials themselves and restrictions in
the use of the subject catalog, in which case a special subject catalog must be maintained. In the event that these materials are ultimately to be incorporated in the general library collection, when
security regulations have been removed, the subject analysis should
be such as to permit incorporation into the general library catalogs
with a minimum of readjustment.

Finally, the fact that any substantive field of knowledge may develop its own theory and history has led to the practice of introducing into bibliothecal classifications symbols representing these two
categories, which may be affixed to any topical symbol in the
scheme. These are not, however, true form categories, but are

rather methods of intellectual manipulation that may be applied to the data of any field.

Form, inasmuch as it relates to properties extrinsic to substantive content, is beyond the scope of the formula for subject analysis. As an instrument of bibliographic classification, such form categories have in the past been regarded largely as a concession to expediency by classifiers who were primarily concerned with the ordering of books as physical objects on library shelves. Books were of necessity arranged according to form when their physical characteristics forced them into nonsubstantive relationships, or when their content transcended the boundaries of single substantive classes. Thus were developed such conventional categories as periodicals, encyclopedias, manuals, etc., or any category based upon physical attributes that might distinguish a book from the norm, e.g., oversize, miniature, or the like.

The subject catalog, unlike shelf classification, divorces the book as a physical entity from its subject content, and therefore it does not need to make any concession to the graphic record as a three-dimensional object. This does not mean, however, that form categories are to be eliminated from the subject catalog. On the contrary, form categories must appear in the subject catalog for two reasons. First, form itself may be represented in the action for which the content of the book stands; or, to state it more colloquially, form may be the "subject" of the book. Thus one may write a book "about" encyclopedias, textbooks, miniature books, poetry, essays, or book illustration.

Second, the inclusion of form categories in the subject catalog may also be a legitimate response to "use or demand." The library clientele may want "a textbook in astronomy," "a chemical formulary," "a dictionary of medical terms," "a bibliography of Elizabethan drama," or "a list of periodicals in sociology." Such requests can be met by the subject catalog only through the inclusion of form categories. Often policies based on more or less arbitrary decisions respecting the treatment of form in the subject catalog can be a real barrier to its most effective utilization; for example, the decision not to analyze fiction according to theme or subject, to indicate literary form only when it is exemplified in the collections or anthologies, to omit categories which might imply criticism of the works to which they would be applied.

It therefore follows that each individual library will have to make its own policy with respect to the extent to which form categories are to be included in the classified catalog. In the present treatment it is possible only to identify certain general considerations respecting which specific decisions must be made. These are included in the body of rules set forth in Section III, which follows.

III. CODE FOR THE CONSTRUCTION AND MAINTENANCE OF A CLASSIFIED CATALOG

A.   Administrative Decisions
Rule 1. Catalog System
     2. General Classification
        System
     3. Special Classifications for
        Particular Subjects
     4. Location Symbols
     5. Special Collections

B.   The Classification System
     6. General Application
     7. Expansion and Revision
     8. Procedure for Expansion
        and Revision
     9. Obsolescence
    10. Crowded Classes
    11. Unused Classes
    12. Relation to the Subject
        Index
    13. Special Schedules
    14. Departures from the
        General System

C.   Classing
    15. Most Probable Use

    16. Permanent Usefulness
    17. Intent of Author
    18. Implied Criticism
    19. Subject of the Whole Work
    20. Coordinate and Compared
        Subjects
    21. Subordinate Subjects
    22. Subject and Form Analytics

D.   The Classified Catalog
    23. Individual Card Entries
    24. Tracing
    25. Guide Cards
    26. Filing
    27. Location of the Catalog
    28. Aids to Users

E.   The Subject Index
    29. Card Form
    30. Withdrawals
    31. Form Subdivision

F.   The Numerial Index to the
        Subject Index File
    32. Preparation and Filing of
        Cards

A. Administrative Decisions

These decisions will be made in the light of the library's defined purposes and scope and the general definition of its readers' needs. They are essential in forming a firm basis for specific decisions on cataloging and classification practice.

1. Catalog System

Determine what types of catalogs are to constitute the whole system and to what extent any of the parts are to be duplicated for various departments. If the classified form is chosen for the subject approach, the subject and numerical indexes, manual of practice, and decisions file should be established immediately. (*Cf.* discussion of the Catalog System, pp.65 ff.)

2. General Classification System

Decide upon the classification system which is to form the basis for the subject analysis of all materials. It may be one of the standard systems — Dewey Decimal, Library of Congress, Universal Decimal, etc. — or a locally devised one. (*Cf.* General Principles for the Construction of a Classification System, p. 22 ff.)

3. Special Classifications for Particular Subjects

In areas of the library's special interest, substitute, when needed, special classifications which are more adequate than those in the general scheme. Segments of a standard large system or specially devised schemes may be used. These may be more specific than the system adopted for general use or organized in a sequence more in harmony with the content of the literature involved or with the viewpoint of users. When such a substitution is adopted, it should be inspected for authority, coverage, continuation, availability in print, etc. Its notation should be such that it may be readily integrated with the general system and mutually exclusive, e.g., in a technological library, substitute Uren, L. C. *Decimal System for Classifying Data Relating to the Petroleum Industry,* Berkeley, Univ. of California Press, 1953, for Dewey Decimal class 665 or Library of Congress classes HD 9560-9580 and TN 860-883.

4. Location Symbols

Decide whether the classification system is to be used for shelving location symbols or exclusively for subject analysis in the classified catalog.
   a. In open-shelf libraries, the class symbol or number becomes a convenient shelving device but if close classification is the established policy, some modification may be necessary for shelving purposes to avoid extremely complex numbers. This is particularly true in the Dewey system. For location symbols, its use should be confined to less than three digits following the decimal point.
   b. In closed-shelf libraries where grouping of materials by subject is not essential, any convenient numbering system may be used, e.g., accession numbers, order numbers, rank shelf scheme, etc.

5. Special Collections

Establish a basic policy for catalog treatment and storage of each type of material requiring segregation because of space considerations, special use, security reasons, stipulations accompanying gift presentations, format of material, etc., e.g., newspapers, microduplicates, ephemeral materials.

    a. Such materials should always be represented in the general catalogs according to the adopted classification scheme even though special indexing is also required. The decision for each type should specify whether the group is to be treated as a whole or each piece cataloged individually; e.g., a portrait collection may be arranged alphabetically by name of subject with a single entry in the classified catalog.

    b. Location of segregated materials should be indicated preferably as part of the call number on all catalog entries and in concise terms that are meaningful to the reader, e.g., Map Room, Patent File, Film Dept.

B. The Classification System

6. General Application

Every entry in the classified catalog should follow the logic of the chosen classification system for all publications, including materials in special and departmental collections. Note that this policy does not preclude the adoption of special classification systems for areas of special interest. In the following rules it is assumed that the greatest degree of specificity is desirable. This is a basic assumption and may be locally modified by administrative decision.

Each class number should include only titles coextensive in coverage with its definition and explicitly named characteristics. Titles covering a broader subject should receive a broader class number. Titles covering only a narrower aspect should receive a more specific class number. This enables the user to define his own searching limits with assurance that he has neither overlooked pertinent materials nor wasted time with the irrelevant.

7. Expansion and Revision

Provide a specific class number for each new focus of interest as need arises; e.g., comparison of class 678 in the 14th and 15th editions of the Dewey Classification illustrates subdivision by subject development.

Making local expansions of the classification system is costly in professional time; hence, such expansions are justified only in the field of the library's special interest. In areas outside that interest, most libraries will use existing schedules without alteration; e.g., a nonagricultural library may find the 637 class of the 15th edition of the Decimal Classification adequate for its materials but a dairy industry library may need all the subdivisions of the 14th edition, and possibly expansions of some of these.

Routines should be established for continual revision and refinement of the classification system, including subdivision of crowded classes, reassignment of unused classes, and correlation of new terms with existing class definitions and the subject index.

8. Procedure for Expansion and Revision

When expansion by further subdivision of a class is needed, proceed as follows:

a. Examine the literature and systematic treatises on the subject to determine usage of specialists in the field. We may assume that the specialist's organization of a subject field is the best outline of a classification plan. It arranges materials in patterns of relationship familiar to the most interested user, i.e., the specialist. It instructs and guides the uninitiated, but interested, user. It does not hamper the casual user.

b. Examine the literature for kinds of form treatment and distinctions arising from use.

c. Examine the literature historically to determine if time and place distinctions are necessary.

d. Examine the terminology of the subject, making certain that terms to be used are discrete and properly defined. Use dictionaries freely, especially dictionaries of the subject.

e. Prepare an outline of the whole subject.

f. Create a glossary of subject headings, including synonyms and inversions.

g. Add notation to preserve the order of the outline determined upon.

h. Inspect older entries in the class being divided for publications which are appropriate to the new subdivisions and subject headings, and transfer their cards to the new class numbers.

i. Enter new subdivisions in the classification schedules, and the subject headings in the subject and numerical indexes.

j. Add a guide card for each class subdivision to the classified catalog.

k. Enter new subdivisions and subject headings, *not immediately used,* in the catalogers' records only; i.e., the classification schedule, catalogers' subject index. Distinguish them by special signals or specially colored cards. Do not enter class or

subject headings in the public catalogs until publications call-
ing for their use are cataloged. *Then* provide subject index
cards to be filed simultaneously with the first classified catalog entry.

9. Obsolescence

Consider the establishment of new outlines, whenever the literature of a subject changes so significantly in vocabulary and direction that the older subdivisions of the class no longer accommodate
publications in meaningful relationships, e.g., Post-Barthian theol-
ogy, or Physics since 1925.

Where a subject is developing rapidly, or new departures in research make it difficult to determine the direction studies will take,
a necessary time lag will often occur. In this case, class a book
where it seems to fit with the older schedules. When the new con-
figurations of the literature become clear and may be outlined, review the older class numbers, and reclassify the publications which
clearly belong in the new outlines. Since new developments generally appear first in journals, a survey of journal articles may guide
the classifier in predicting trends of growth.

Until about 1940, investigations of nuclear phenomena were
largely in the field of physical chemistry. Subsequent developments have been largely in nuclear physics. Hence, with the
publication of the 15th edition of the DC, it becomes necessary
to scrutinize the titles classified previously in 541, and to transfer some to 539. Similarly, materials classed in 577 PROPER-
TIES OF LIVING MATTER (14th ed.) should be examined to
choose and transfer those belonging in 574.1 BIOCHEMISTRY
and 574.191 BIOPHYSICS (15th ed.).

Dyson, F. W. *Determination of the deflection of light by the
sun's gravitational field from observations made at the total
eclipse of May 29, 1919.* Washington, Smithsonian Inst., 1921.
(an early demonstration of relativity)
  This might have been classed, when it appeared, 535.1
THEORY OF LIGHT, or 523.78 SOLAR ECLIPSES. If so, it
should, with our present knowledge, be transferred to 530.12
RELATIVITY.

Include provision for the older literature in the new outlines, so
that its relationships are preserved and its interest to the new materials indicated, e.g., works in medieval alchemy of importance to
modern chemistry.

10. Crowded Classes

When the number of entries within a given class becomes too large for efficient manipulation, consider the advisability of subdivision.

11. Unused Classes

When inspection reveals that no new material has been entered in a class for some years, investigate the reason. It may be necessary to:
   a. Abolish the class and to reclassify publications entered there, in classes where they will be more useful, or
   b. Redefine the class and to include publications which have been wrongly classed elsewhere.

12. Relation to the Subject Index

For each class number in the classified catalog establish one or more corresponding and synonymous subject headings. No term in the subject index should refer to a class broader than the term. Thus: class number = subject heading and subject heading = class number. (*Cf*. Rule 29.)

        551.5   METEOROLOGY
        551.59   CLIMATE
        551.591   WEATHER
              not
        551.5   CLIMATE
        551.5   WEATHER

Similarly, no term in the subject index should be broader than the class number to which it refers, e.g., ARTERIES — ANATOMY, 611.13 and ARTERIES — DISEASES, 616.13, not ARTERIES, 611.13 and 616.13.

If it is impossible to immediately determine the correct relationship of a new subject to its field, provide a temporary entry in the subject indexes with the class symbol of the nearest inclusive class. This practice should always be regarded as extremely temporary and provision made for thorough treatment at the earliest possible moment.

A commonly used alternative to further subdivision of the notation is to arrange cards alphabetically by subject within the larger group, using appropriate guide cards. A symbol to indicate such

> BERYLLIUM POISONING
>
> 615.925 (Metallic poisoning)

arrangement should be added wherever the class number appears, i.e., classification schedule, subject index entries, etc.

615.925   METALLIC POISONING
615.925 [1] ALUMINUM POISONING
615.925 [1] BERYLLIUM POISONING

13. Special Schedules

When special schedules are substituted for a part of the general classification, use the notation of the substituted schedule with as little change as possible. This preserves the virtues of the special schedule, and makes additions and revisions simpler as they appear in print.

14. Departures from the General System

When exceptions are made to the general policy of classification:
a. Record the exceptions in the Decisions File, e.g., the degree of application of form symbols.
b. Supply copies to *all* classifiers.
c. Indicate these decisions in the catalogers' subject index, the classification schedules, and numerical index.

C. Classing

15. Most Probable Use

This will require consideration of the library's purposes and the needs of the users, so far as they can be defined. The logic of the classification system must at some times give way to the defined purpose of the library; e.g., in a technological library, where fine arts are considered "out of scope," GLASS GRINDING AND POLISHING is classed in 666.1 (Glass manufacture) rather than 748.16 (Decorative art).

16. Permanent Usefulness

Class a book, so far as is possible, according to its permanent usefulness rather than its immediate impact. (*Cf.* Rule 9).

17. Intent of Author

Consider the intent of the author as a major indication of the usefulness of the publication.
Exceptions: Where the data presented outweigh in value the thesis the author intends to prove, class by subject of the data, e.g., class Pohl, J. F. *The Kenny concept of infantile paralysis.* Minneapolis, Bruce, 1943, in 616.8321, POLIOMYELITIS rather than in 615.832, HEAT THERAPY.

In older materials the author's purpose may have lost its interest, while the data presented take first place in the use of the materials; e.g., for the Domesday book, prefer 942.01, GREAT BRITAIN — HISTORY — SOURCES to 342.02, GREAT BRITAIN — TAXATION.

18. Implied Criticism

Avoid a classification which expresses an implied criticism on the part of the classifier, rather than an objectively observed characteristic of the publication; e.g., class unorthodox medical literature by subject, regardless of theories advanced.

19. Subject of the Whole Work

Class each publication in the most specific class which describes its content *as a whole;* e.g., in a general library:

> 338.17361
>   Sitterson, J. C.
>   *Sugar country: the cane sugar industry in the*
>   *South, 1753-1950.* [Lexington, Univ. of Kentucky
>   Press, 1953]

In special libraries, the whole may be interpreted as being only that portion of the book which is of interest to the user of the special

collection; e.g., above example classed in 633.61, SUGAR CULTIVA-
TION.

20. Coordinate and Compared Subjects

Class a publication treating two or more subjects coordinately
or comparatively in the most specific classes which describe *each*
of those subjects.

    546.28 [SILICON]
International Union of Chemistry. Section for
   Inorganic Chemistry.
      Silicon -- sulphur -- phosphates: colloquium.
   Münster, Verlag Chemie, 1955.

      546.22 [SULPHUR] 546.18 [PHOSPHORUS]

Note that the class number 546.1 would represent this book as a
treatise on nonmetallic inorganic chemistry, which it is not.

In cases where specific class numbers for several subjects
treated coordinately would have little value, class the publication
in the number for the nearest inclusive group.

    615.8 [PHYSIOTHERAPY]
Kovacs, Richard.
      Nature, M. D.; healing forces of heat, water,
   light, electricity and exercise. New York,
   London, D. Appleton-Century, 1934.

---

21. Subordinate Subjects

Make additional class entries for each subordinate or contribut-
ing subject in a publication if it has significant value to the user of
the literature. Such subjects may be:

a. A contribution to the understanding of the main subject.

---

677 [TEXTILES]
Kaswell, Ernest R.
   Textile fibers, yarns and fabrics; a comparative
survey of their behavior with special reference to
wool. New York, Reinhold, 1953.

677.98 [WOOL FABRICS]

---

b. A methodology for the main subject.

545.836 [PAPER CHROMATOGRAPHY]
Linskens, H   F   , ed.
   Papierchromatographie in der Botanik. Berlin,
Springer, 1955.

581.104 [PLANTS — PHYSIOLOGY]

---

c. A conclusion drawn from the investigation.

532.6 [CAPILLARITY]
Manegold, Erich.
   Kapillarsysteme. Heidelberg, Chemie und
Technik Verlagsgesellschaft, 1955.

620.1122 [TESTS OF SURFACE WEATHERING]

---

22. Subject and Form Analytics

Make an entry in the classified catalog for any portion of a work
different from the whole in either form or subject matter whenever
that portion is important to the total literature of the subject. In

the field of the library's special subject interest a minor section
may assure major importance.

923.242 [ENGLISH STATESMEN]
Clarendon, Edward Hyde, 1st earl of, 1609-1674.
 The life of Edward, earl of Clarendon ...
Oxford, Clarendon Printing House, 1759.
 Contains first known account of the symptoms
of angina pectoris (v. 1, p. 16-18)

616.127 [ANGINA PECTORIS]

If evidence of intent, as stated by the author or in content of a
bibliography, indicates that it will serve as a general summary of
the literature on the subject treated, a classified catalog entry
should be made for the bibliography.

641.326 [ANIMAL FOODS]
Bodenheimer, Friedrich Simon.
 Insects as food; a chapter on the ecology of
man. The Hague, W. Junk, 1951.
 Bibliography: p. 331-350.

591.63 [ECONOMIC ZOOLOGY] 016.641326
[ANIMAL FOODS — BIBLIOGRAPHY]

D. The Classified Catalog

The classified catalog is made up of individual cards for materials classified and guide cards bearing class symbols, subject
headings, scope notes, and indications of the method of arrangement.

23. Individual Card Entries

Each card entered in the classified catalog should include the
class number assigned, location symbol (call number), and bibliographic identification of the item. Descriptive cataloging is not

discussed in this manual. It is assumed that entries will take the
form prescribed by standard cataloging practice. They may vary
from complete detailed description to the briefest possible identification, depending on local decision.

```
                                                              TElb
         677.98                                               291
      Alexander, Peter, 1922-
         Wool; its chemistry and physics, by Peter Alexander
      and Robert F. Hudson.  New York, Reinhold, 1954.
         viii, 404 p.  illus.




         I. Hudson, Robert Francis, joint author.  677.98
      ICJ55 O
      322674
                                O
```

---

24. Tracing

Record, on at least one copy of each set of cards, all entries
made for that title, including those in the author-title catalog and
the classified catalog. This card then becomes the "main entry."
It is usually the author card, but may be the shelf-list card or any
other convenient entry. If the unit card system is used in cataloging, the identification of a "main entry" is unnecessary.

25. Guide Cards

A guide card should be provided for each major class number
and for as many subdivisions as the accumulation of cards warrants.
If the classification symbol is omitted from individual cards, a
guide card must be made *for every variation* in the classification
symbol. It should be made when the class number is first assigned
and filed simultaneously with the first entry.
  a. A guide card should always include the class number and sub-
     ject heading and scope or reference notes when appropriate.
  b. Where large groups of cards accumulate in one class number,
     subordinate date or alphabetical guide cards should be placed
     at intervals (e.g., every inch) to facilitate location.

517.7 CALCULUS — OPERATIONAL
METHODS

Includes Fourier integrals, Fourier and
Laplace transformations

c. Guide cards for form subdivisions should be distinctive from
   subject and date guides in color of ink, card stock, or position.
d. Guide cards should show the structure of the class and the degree of subdivision by means of graduated position, varying
   color, type or card stock. Since both class numbers and subject headings tend to grow in length with increasing specificity,
   care in the choice of the physical guide will be necessary to
   make clear the class structure, and to provide sufficient
   space for long headings.

624		STRUCTURAL ENGINEERING
.06		Societies
.15		FOUNDATIONS, EARTHWORK
	.151	ENGINEERING SOILS
	.152	TUNNELING
.16		RETAINING WALLS
.17		THEORY OF STRUCTURE
	.171	STRESS ANALYSIS
	.177	DESIGN OF STRUCTURAL ELEMENTS
	.1771	BEAMS
	.1776	TRUSSES
	.1777	FRAMES AND FRAMING

e. Scope notes, by defining the coverage and viewpoint of the
   class, are helpful to the user and an aid to consistency in
   classifying. They should appear on the face of the guide
   card and be identical with those on subject and numerical
   index entries. If long, a scope note may appear on a separate card immediately following the guide card. A distinguishing color of card stock for such cases will call them to
   the attention of the user and prevent misplacement in subsequent filing.

26. Filing

File cards in the classified catalog by class number, in the

order of the classification system. Within each class number, file
individual cards by:

a. Author or entry word [not recommended] or
b. Date of publication, in chronological, or reverse chronological order [recommended]

Particularly for a technical or scientific library, it is desirable
to give prominence to the most recent materials. Choice of filing
policy should be established on the basis of local needs and the
scope of the collection. Any variation from the general filing policy
should be signaled with a special guide card to warn both user and
filer.

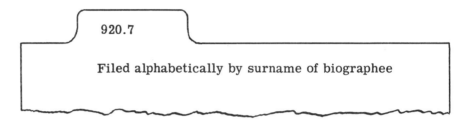

920.7

Filed alphabetically by surname of biographee

27. Location of the Catalog

The subject index should be placed as close as possible to the
classified catalog and the author-title catalog should be so located
as to make possible the greatest freedom of movement from one to
the other.

28. Aids to Users

Outlines of the classification system should be displayed near
the classified catalog. In a special library of limited scope, these
may be more detailed within the areas of special emphasis. Copies
of the complete classification schedules should be readily available
to users.

E. The Subject Index

29. Card Form

For each class number used provide cards under every appropriate term and its synonyms, giving the corresponding class number in the classified catalog and a word or phrase indicating the
larger category in which the classification falls. (*Cf.* Rule 12.)

CAMEL'S HAIR

    677.34 (Textile manufactures)

---

or

CAMEL'S HAIR: TEXTILE MANUFACTURES 677.34

Note: This variant form, though equally adequate, is not repeated
in examples of succeeding rules.

  a. In many cases the same subject heading will cover materials
in more than one class number. In this case, give, on a single
card, all class numbers, each with the explanatory phrase.
For convenience, arrange the numbers on each card in classification order. Explanatory phrases accompanying class symbols should identify for the user the phase of the subject covered. In most cases, the terminology of the preceding major
class in the classification scheme will suffice.

BEANS

            583.22 (Botany)
            633.3 (Field crops)
            635.65 (Horticulture)

---

  b. When a class number is used for the first time, the books
classed there and lists of subject headings should be searched
for synonyms, and a subject index card made for each synonym
and inversion, referring to the class number. No "see" references appear in the subject index; each synonym and inversion
refers directly to the class number, e.g., one card for each:

DOMESTIC ECONOMY	640 (Homemaking)
DOMESTIC SCIENCE	640 (Homemaking)
HOME ECONOMICS	640 (Homemaking)
HOME MAKING	640 (Home management)
HOMEMAKING	640 (Home management)
HOUSEHOLD MANAGEMENT	640 (Homemaking)
HOUSEKEEPING	640 (Homemaking)

Note that a separate card is made for each of these terms, and copies filed alphabetically in the subject index. In the numerical index, however, all terms relating to a given class symbol may be combined on one or more cards.

    c. When a new class number is used for a subject already entered in the subject index, either replace all copies of the card with new ones having both old and new class numbers, each with explanatory phrase, or have the new number and phrase added to all copies.

    d. When scope notes are necessary to define the limits of a class symbol, the same note should appear on all subject and numerical index cards. (*Cf.* Rule 25e.)

30. Withdrawals

    a. When a class is abolished in the classified catalog, withdraw from the subject and numerical indexes all subject index cards referring to that number. These may be traced by means of the numerical index. Care should be taken that all synonymous terms are withdrawn.

    b. If a subject index card includes two or more class numbers, one of which is abolished, remake the subject index card, omitting the abolished number. In this case, the catalogers' subject index entry should retain the reference to the abolished number with the reason for cancellation.

31. Form Subdivision

When a form subdivision is used with a class number, include the subject heading with subdivision and subdivided class number in the subject and numerical indexes.

MINING ENGINEERING — SOCIETIES — GERMANY

622.0643 (Mining)

F. The Numerical Index to the Subject Index File

A tracing file, arranged in the order of the chosen classification system, must include every class number used and every term in the subject index.

32. Preparation and Filing of Cards

Numerical index cards may be either duplicates of cards in the subject index or one or more cards listing all synonymous terms used in the subject index. The former method has the distinct advantage of convenience in making additions; the latter conserves space. (*Cf.* Rule 29b.) If duplicates of subject index cards are used underscore or circle the filing number when more than one class symbol appears on the card.

CANCELLARIIDAE

     564.32 (Paleontology)
     594.32 (Zoology)

Appendix A

Method for the systematic analysis
of materials to be classed

Because the classified catalog offers the opportunity to use the terms of the classification system to describe individual character- istics that are only one part of the total description of the book, the analysis of the book must bring out clearly and consistently such significant characteristics rather than merely suggest alternative classes that represent the book as a whole.

Instruction in the art of classifying has in general been so closely associated with the use of one of the traditional, generally accepted, classification systems that it has consisted almost en- tirely of the interpretation of the schedule of the system, with prac- tice in the actual placing of materials and the analysis of particular problems that arise within the context of that system. Emphasis has inevitably been upon the choice of the one class within which the book was to be physically placed.

Today, when so many library systems demand the construction and use of special classification systems, and when the old hier- archical systems seem to be giving way to multidimensional sys- tems with their poles, or axes, chosen according to local needs, a new approach to the intellectual analysis of materials to be classi- fied is urgently needed. Such a method of analysis should start with the materials themselves and the categories of characteristics which they evince. The accurate perception of such characteristics and a firm hand in harnessing them together is the basis for placing materials rationally and consistently in an existing system.

The necessity for the development of such a methodology was pointed out by Shera in his "Classification as the Basis of Organization."[1] There have been, in the recent past, several attempts to apply this approach to particular schema, situations, or subject fields, the most general of which are Ranganathan's development of the five "facets" for the analysis of materials, in connection with his Colon Classification,[2] and Bliss's attempt to correlate the various "orders" in his Synoptic Tables.[3] Other attempts have been limited largely to the fields of science and technology. An attempt is made in the following pages to derive a general formula that will direct the classifier's attention *away* from consideration of the book as an exemplification of *singleness* of the author's purpose and *toward* all the constituent elements which may be of predictable use to any reader.[4]

In grammatical syntax sentence structure may be presented in completely abstract terms, thus providing a mold into which every complete statement may be fitted regardless of its substantive content. A similar construct for the analysis of abstract relations may be seen in geometry, which has been generalized into formal propositions without reference to actual measurements, distances, or numerical coordinates for the indication of points. The distinctive feature of each system is that it presents a pattern of *relationships* in which the relata are expressed in abstract terms, for which may be substituted any concrete term, the terms varying appropriately with every particular problem or situation. So, likewise, it should be possible to discover a group of generalized relationships among the characteristics of bibliographic units, wherein the relata would be the essential elements of the activity of which the book is a record. It is important to note in this connection that the relata

---

[1] Jesse H. Shera and Margaret E. Egan, eds., *Bibliographic Organization* (Chicago: University of Chicago Press, 1951), pp.83-88.

[2] *Op. cit.*, pp.94-105.

[3] Henry E. Bliss, *The Organization of Knowledge* (New York: Henry Holt, 1929), pp.229-35.

[4] The initial stages of this work owe much to Eaton's attempt to clarify semantic difficulties by devising general categories of words according to their function in the expression of thought or action. The context of her work was the single sentence — the smallest unit of thought — while ours is the bibliothecal unit, which may be of any size or complexity, but the general formula of analysis is very similar. Cf. Helen Eaton, *Semantic Frequency List for English, French, German, and Spanish* (Chicago: University of Chicago Press, 1940), table in Appendix.

express *function* in a particular context, that they do not themselves provide a basis for classification on the principle of *inherent like-nesses* or *differentia.*

Inasmuch as the rules for classifying, or for constructing sub-ject headings, usually arise from *problems of relationship* among such elements, it may be assumed that codes of such rules or deci-sions will reveal the major problems confronting classifiers. An initial analysis of the problems of relationship set forth in Merrill's *Code for Classifiers*[5] and the Vatican Code[6] revealed that these problems group themselves into a limited number of problem types. These were first identified as:

> Problem complex vs. subject discipline
> Inter-subject relations
> Material used as data for more than one subject
> Relationship between theory and application or practice
> Art or technology in relation to product
> Activity or event in relation to protagonist or person(s)
>   involved
> Product in relation to use
> Subject — place
> Subject — time
> Subject — object
> Process — tool
> Material — process
> Form — subject

In the first analysis Literature and Music were omitted because they seemed to present problems different in *kind,* but further study disclosed that the differences were more apparent than real, and problems from both areas were fitted easily into the final pattern.

Each of the problems classified into these thirteen groups was composed of a variety of constituent elements. In most of the ex-amples the problem arose from a conflict between two elements for primacy in emphasis, although in some cases the conflict in-volved three or more elements. In the construction of a classified catalog such a conflict loses its importance, for it is possible to make an entry for each element. Even in libraries where books are arranged on shelves according to the primary class number, the choice of primary class is frequently an arbitrary one based

---

[5]William S. Merrill, *Code for Classifiers* (Chicago: American Library Association, 1939).

[6]Vatican. Biblioteca Vaticana, *Rules of the Catalog,* Wyllis E. Wright, ed. (Chicago: American Library Association, 1948).

upon untested assumptions of use and relying upon the subject catalog to bring out other relations. In libraries with closed stacks relying entirely upon the catalog for subject access, shelf arrangement is inconsequential. The value of systematic analysis lies not
in determining a *single* most desirable class (the object of most
rules of classification) but rather in achieving *maximum utility
with the least number of entries*. The crux of the problem, then,
is to ensure systematic consideration of each potentially useful element in the work to be classified rather than to resolve conflicts
for primacy.

A summary of the elements appearing anywhere in the original
analysis of such conflicts is surprisingly brief and discloses the
fact that some of them arise through the use of terms at different
levels of organization. Still others coalesce as parts of the same
concept when they are considered in relation to function rather
than intrinsic property. The final list of functionally different elements thus emerges:

Subject, used in two senses: (1) a protag- **AGENT**
       onist or active agent, e.g., the
       subject of a biography; (2) see
       below.
Protagonist

Process
Activity, or event, usually appearing as ACT
       a substantive term covering all
       aspects of a process or act.

Theory, used in two meanings: (1) an INSTRUMENTALITY
       abstract principle or generali-
       zation concerning a specific
       body of data, being itself the
       product of the scientist's study
       of the data but appearing in
       problems of classification as
       opposed to the use made of it in
       applied science or technology;
       (2) see below.
Tool, or equipment
Data, a body of facts which may be studied
       or used from any point of view
       or in any one of several contexts.

Material, substance used in performing
      the act or process but not the
      direct object upon which work
      is performed.

Object, that which is acted upon, whether   OBJECT
      tangible or intangible, including
Material, when it is directly acted upon.

Time   **TIME**

Place, locus   **SPACE**

Product, that which emerges as a result   **PRODUCT**
      of the entire process, either
      tangible or intangible

Subject, (2) in the sense of a field of study or academic discipline.

Theory, (2) that part of a subject field which consists of a body of related abstract principles or generalizations, appearing in classification problems as "pure" vs. "applied" sciences.

Art or Technology, a body of knowledge relating to "how-to-do something," usually derived from practical experience but sometimes depending in part upon abstract principles derived from one of the sciences or subject fields.

Problem complex, a situation involving a number of elements which must be treated from the point of view, or with the techniques, of several of the sciences or technologies. Sometimes represents the first stages of a developing subject field or technology. Differs from activity or event both in magnitude and in the fact that study

Each of these terms is a broad, substantive designation applied to a sequence or cluster of related and interdependent acts. When possible, analysis should be specific as to the *particular* acts. When, however, these terms appear as integral units of thought the whole takes its place functionally as object, product, or instrumentality in the act or context in which it appears.

of it is oriented toward a definite
goal or result whereas the event
or activity may be completely
accidental in the elements it
brings together.

———

Use, employed here not in the sense of the use expected to be
made of the book, but rather to indicate a content
which explicitly discusses the use or employment of
certain means by certain individuals or groups, e.g.,
"The Use of Radio in Advertising" or "Accounting for
Retail Stores." Here, the act or process described is
carried out by advertisers or retail storekeepers, and
there is no functional difference from the category
"Agent." Use therefore either disappears from the
problem elements or may be expressed in a separate
cycle of analysis.

Form, a category which refers directly to the graphic record
itself and its physical attributes, rather than to content.
This element, accordingly, is omitted from the formula
for subject analysis, and is dealt with separately in
Chapter 3, Section II, D. The Category of Form p. 84.

The final step in the evolution of an abstract formula for analysis of subject content grows out of recognition of the fact that every
written record is the record of an *act,* and therefore the separately
identifiable elements of a complete act are the essential ingredients
to be identified in the analysis of the subject content of books or
records. The act may be physical or mental, simple or complex,
explicitly containing all, or a limited number, of the elements im-
plicitly present in the complete formula. An important phase of
analysis is the ability to discern factors that are implicit rather
than explicit, thus facilitating comprehension of the function of
the elements explicitly present. In other words, the *act* is the
unit of thought and it may appear at any level of organization,
with its factors simple or complex, according to the context in
which it is treated (cf. pp. 25-27).

A. Formula for Analysis of Content

AGENT - ACT - INSTRUMENTALITIES - OBJECT - TIME -
(performs) (with)   (upon)   (in)   (in)
SPACE - PRODUCT
(yielding) (used by ...)

AGENT (new cycle begins here, with the "product" of the above
cycle taking its place as agent, instrumentality, or object
in this cycle)

Upon first inspection, the list of essential elements of the formula may seem to be too limited to be applicable to all possible
situations. Yet, when the separate terms have been completely defined and the extension of each systematically explored, their adequacy may be successfully demonstrated by testing them against a
body of materials drawn from a variety of subject fields. Before
attempting to apply the formula as a whole, then, it is necessary
to explain the meaning and scope of each separate term.

Agent: That which initiates, directs, performs, or shapes the
act. It may be personal or impersonal, tangible or intangible, individual or collective.

Examples:

national leader	chemical solvent
scientist	electrical impulse
technician	corporation
artist	association
social myth	national government
national ideal	race
moral habit	religious group

Act: That which is done or performed; the exercise of power or
influence; the bringing about of an effect. The act may be single,
multiple, or composite. When multiple or composite it may be
termed a *process.* The process, regardless of the number of separate steps or length of time involved, may be held to be an act when
it is considered in its entirety or as a unified whole.

Examples:

to manufacture	to classify
to govern	to imagine
to invent	to create
to study	to mold
to describe	to influence

Instrumentality: That which serves as a means to the *agent* in
the execution of the *act.* It may be tangible or intangible, human or
nonhuman, material or methodological.

Note: Method is used to denote a particular way of performing an act or process, similar to skill or technique. It thus appears frequently as instrumentality when knowledge of a particular method is essential to the process, but it may also appear occasionally as object or product when the act performed is the act of devising or improving a method as an end in itself; e.g., Statistician develops *method of sampling*

Examples:
> methods of analysis in statistics, chemistry, etc.
> mathematical symbols or representation
> tools and equipment
> ideas or theories
> chemical reagents
> social organizations; schools; institutions, etc.
> human beings; actors, officers, etc.

Object: That which is worked upon by the *agent* through the *act* by means of the instrumentality; it is the antithesis of the agent and differs from the instrumentality in that some change must be brought about in the object itself or in the agent's comprehension of the object; e.g., Scientist studies atom. It has no properties as object apart from its direct relation to the agent or the act.

Examples:
> public opinion or attitudes
> scientific theories
> chemical substances
> architectural structures
> literary or historical periods
> machines
> raw materials essential to product

Time: The measurable aspect of duration within which the change is accomplished. For purposes of classification different scales of time will be necessary for different purposes. Universal history must be measured in large units; chemical or physical reactions require minute and very precise measurements. Duration or point of time is frequently irrelevant in classification but adds a dimension that is one source of confusion when it conflicts with other dimensions such as space.

Examples:
> U. S. History. Colonial, 1602-1775
> English History. Stuart period, 1603-1714

World War I
    Events of 1914
    Events of 1915
    Events of 1916
French Literature. Classical period, 1600-1715
Hours of work. Portal-to-portal allowances
Time records
Timing of photographic processes

Space: The physical locus within which the act takes place.
Space is an inclusive term of undetermined dimensions within which
any number of loci may occur. As in the case of time the schedule
of classification will vary in magnitude according to need. Considerations of space may also be irrelevant in many contexts.

Examples:
    Geographic areas   Dramatic unity of place
        Western Hemisphere   Drawingroom scene
        Indian Ocean   Battlefield
    Political divisions   Ecological regions
        Mexico   Corn belt
        Boston   Fishing banks
    Topographic features   Administrative units
        Pike's Peak   Plant or branch of company
        Ohio River   School or institution

Product: That which results from the *act,* whether of generation,
growth, labor, thought, or influence. The product of one act may become the agent, the instrumentality, or the object of one or more
succeeding cycles.

Examples:
    steam engine   chemical compounds
    binomial theorem   literary creation
    theory of evolution   national foreign policy
    law of diminishing   artistic creation
        returns   criminal law
    farm crops   public opinion

Any term of the formula, or any selected cluster of such terms,
may represent the focus of attention, or axis of emphasis, of any
given library. Some libraries may deal with a universe so limited
that it is desirable to emphasize only one of the terms. Thus a
metallurgical library might concentrate upon the characteristics
or properties of metals as the *Object* or thing worked upon, with

subordinate attention to *Act* or to *Process* or *Instrumentalities*. *Example. Merrill 215, Radio.*

Merrill gives four classes of works under *Radio:*

a. Works on the construction of the radio and its accessories. The titles he cites here are *Radio Construction and Repairing* and *The Radio Antenna Handbook*. From the meager information given in these titles it is possible to recognize certain of the elements which would be part of a total analysis suggested in the outline of the table presented above. The "act or process" is explicitly construction and repair, and the "product" is a working radio. The "agent" may be assumed to be radio engineers or technicians; the "tools" and "materials" are not specified in the titles, but a considerable list of each could no doubt be derived from the books themselves. How many and which of these should be brought out in any particular catalog will depend upon the nature of the library, the extent of its resources, and its clientele. Inasmuch as the emphasis of these books is undoubtedly upon "process" if but one class is to be assigned to these titles, they would be classed simply as "Radio Engineering." The number of additional classes to be assigned will vary in extent with the level of analysis desired. In present use, the elements of "time" and "space" are not important. If at some future time these books should be held to be important for a study of the development of radio technology, classification symbols representing these elements would be assigned to these titles in the catalog.

b. Works on special uses and applications of the radio. The titles cited here are:

1. *Safety of Life at Sea Through the Use of Radio*
2. *A Decade of Radio Advertising*
3. *Present and Pending Applications to Education of Radio and Allied Arts*
4. *Men and Radio Music*

In at least three of these examples the emphasis is again upon "process." Appropriate entries being, respectively, Safeguarding Life, Advertising, and Education. The content of the fourth is less clearly indicated by the title. It may be assumed, however, for purposes of illustration that it is a study of the effect of radio music upon men. In this instance the formula might read: Radio music (agent) affects (process) men (object) with what result (product). The product may be increased appreciation, increased stereotyping of taste, or debasing of taste, but in any case the question of the effect upon men appears to be the crucial point of the book.

c. Works on the technique of broadcasting. No titles are cited but Radio Engineering is suggested as the general class under which this topic falls. Obviously, then, the mechanical or technical aspect of broadcasting is the process in which radio is the instrumentality used, those who operate the broadcasting equipment the agent, and the finished broadcast is the product.

d. Works on the writing of plays for broadcasting by radio. The titles cited here are: *Learn to Write for Broadcasting* and *Writing for Broadcasting.* Writing, in the sense of literary composition, is the process, the product is explicitly the script of the radio play, and it is explicitly to be used for radio programming. It is obvious here that the agent is the author and the material may vary from a concrete and very real historical incident to the most imaginative fantasy.

These four classes would be diagrammed as shown on page 115.

Here again it must be emphasized that the formula is not itself a classification system or even the basis upon which a classification system can be built. It is a *pattern of analysis* that does no more than propound the basic question which every classifier of bibliographical units must ask — Who does what to what with what instrumentalities with what result? Having thus analyzed the materials in these terms, the task of their appropriate organization still remains. Each of the terms of the formula, or question, therefore admits of reference to an almost unlimited number of independent classification systems based upon properties or characteristics inherent in the things classified regardless of function in any particular context or situation.

In the example of the metallurgical library given above, metals would be exhaustively classified according to their own intrinsic properties so that it would be possible to refer to any single metal by its distinctive class symbol and to any property it might possess. It would be impracticable, however, to include an added entry for every instance in which a particular metal is mentioned. To achieve optimum utility with the minimum number of entries, each metal would be considered in relation to its function and the importance of that function in a particular context.

It therefore becomes the first responsibility of the librarian in selecting or devising a classification scheme for his own institution to analyze the graphic records with which he is concerned in terms

Merrill 215 RADIO

AGENT (performs) →	ACT (with) →	TOOLS (upon) →	OBJECT (in) →	TIME (in) →	SPACE (resulting in) →	PRODUCT (useful to or used by) →	AGENT ... (begins new cycle)
Animate or inanimate Individual or group	Process or method (a particular organization or process)	Instrumentalities, animate or inanimate	Materials (inanimate) Persons (animate)			Tangible or intangible	
a.	Construction Repair						
b.	Safeguarding life	Radio					
	Advertising	Radio					
	Educating	Radio	Men				
c.	Broadcasting (technical)	Radio				Radio	
d.	Writing					Plays	Radio program planners

of the formula and to interpret the foci of attention of his clientele
with respect to those elements of the formula that will become the
axes of emphasis. Such a procedure builds a solid foundation for
future consistency in classing materials, for it establishes a given
order of priority in directing attention to the chosen elements without precluding the exercise of individual judgment as to whether or
not the element is represented in a particular document significantly enough to justify classification.

The applicability of the formula to the pure and applied sciences
is obvious, but it is equally valuable as a tool of analysis in the humanities. As Allen Tate recently said, "It may be said at once that
art being a form of conduct... What we are confronted with in a
work of literature, and I suppose also in the other arts, is human
action translated into *being* ..."[7] In general, the creative works
that are the heart of the humanistic studies may be schematized:

AGENT	ACT	INSTRUMENTALITIES	OBJECT	PRODUCT
Artist	Interprets	Data from	(Usually un-	Poem
		Sensual experience	important)	Novel
		Imagination	Paper	Symphony
		Techniques	Canvas	Painting
		Skill in prosody	Stone	Ballet
		Knowledge of harmony	etc.	Statue
		etc.		etc.

The primary focus of attention in these fields is obviously the
Product, with the Agent a second focus of considerable, if varying,
attention. While the instrumentalities at the command of an artist
and his skill in using them receive much critical attention, in the
context of criticism they are considered as attributes of the artist
as agent and even serve as the principle for classifying artists into
schools or classes. Critical works may be schematized:

AGENT	ACT	INSTRUMENTALITIES	OBJECT	PRODUCT
Critic	Appraises	Generally accepted	Poem	An interpreta-
		standards	Novel	tion or evalua-
		Subjective reactions	Symphony	tion which may
			Painting	itself become
			Ballet	an instrument
			Statue	in shaping the
			etc.	aesthetic judg-
				ment of a peo-
				ple or a gener-
				ation.

[7]Allen Tate, "The Self-Made Angel," *New Republic*, 129 (Aug. 31, 1953), p.17.

B. The Cyclical Aspects of Analysis

By far the greatest proportion of classification problems arise from the "interrelatedness" of phenomena and therefore of graphic records. No situation, no phenomenon, and no document ever exists without ties of some kind that extend beyond the boundaries of its own existence. Fortunately, some of these ties or bonds are unimportant for practical purposes, but in many instances comprehension of the bond or relationship is the *sine qua non* of effective classification. Not all of these bonds are explicit in the simple application of the formula; many extend beyond the immediate situation. Though every document or graphic record must necessarily first be analyzed in terms of the formula, every document exists in, and has relationships with, milieu which itself involves relationships that are repetitive, sequential, cyclical. It is therefore necessary that the formula reflect this cyclical character of the entire situation in which human knowledge and experience and the graphic records of that knowledge and experience exist. That the formula can be repeatedly applied in a cyclical manner has been suggested above, but it is desirable to make more explicit here the exact nature of application in a small sample of those situations where it is appropriate. It should also be noted that the interdependence of the cycles may assume a variety of forms (patterns) or functions, but each cycle is a focal point with multiple antecedents and multiple consequences, as shown on pages 118 and 119.

Whenever possible the content of a single bibliographic unit should be expressed within the framework of a single cycle. When this cannot be done, the fewest possible number of cycles should be used. Intensity of analysis may be achieved not only through increasing the number of cycles employed to describe the action represented in the bibliographic unit, but also through increasing the number of items listed under each element of the formula. Thus, in the examples given here it is obvious that the list of factors itemized under *Instrumentality, Object,* etc. might be extended. The degree of specificity employed will depend upon the level of analysis desired, and will, of course, vary from library to library and bibliographic unit to bibliographic unit.

C. Application of the Formula

What has been said in the preceding pages concerning the nature of the formula as an instrument of analysis suggests with reasonable clarity the method and technique of its application to any particular problem in classification or to any specific title to be analyzed as to subject content. In general the application of the formula has been

Author — writes — Knowledge of country or region — Novel (About Social conditions in country or region)

Nature and Society | shapes *Biological* Heredity Genes *Social* Education | Man (author with certain characteristics)

Physical factors and Social factors | shape | Country or Region (Geographic and Social characteristics)

Novel — instigates — Social consciousness — Reform of Social conditions in country or region

Novel — arouses — Readers — Interest in Social conditions

Critics — appraise — Novel — Value of Novel as social document / Literary excellence and maturity of Novel

AGENT	ACT	OBJECT	PRODUCT
Scientists	study	Metals	Knowledge about nature and properties of Metals (Metallurgy)

AGENT	ACT	INSTRUMENTALITY	OBJECT	PRODUCT
Technicians	Manufacture (i.e., temper harden, etc.)	Knowledge of Metallurgy plus Practical experience	Metal	Metal manufacture

AGENT	ACT	INSTRU- MENTALITY	OBJECT	PRODUCT
Farmers	produce	Soil	Crops Livestock	Agricultural produce Soil erosion

AGENT	ACT	INSTRUMENTALITY	OBJECT	PRODUCT
Farmers and Engineers	Control	Contouring reforestation flood control etc.	Soil erosion	Soil conservation

AGENT	ACT	OBJECT	PRODUCT
Constitution	confers powers upon	Court	Politically active agent in society (e.g., the Court)

AGENT	ACT	OBJECT	PRODUCT
The Court	renders decision upon	Actual problem	Regulation of social conduct

found to be a relatively simple operation, but there are instances in which difficulties may arise.

Perhaps the greatest problem for the beginner lies in the predisposition to confuse the aspect of reality that the book reflects (the real focus of attention in the application of the formula) with the aspect of reality that the book itself *is:* Thus at the outset one may find himself repeatedly writing such analyses as:

AGENT	ACT	INSTRUMENTALITY	OBJECT	PRODUCT
Author	writes history	using historical data	Wat Tyler's Rebellion	history of rebellion

when the correct analysis of such a title should read:

AGENT	ACT	INSTRUMEN- TALITY	OBJECT	SPACE	TIME	PRODUCT
Wat Tyler	incites	general discontent with heavy taxation	peasants	England	13th cent.	revolt

The action recorded in the formula, therefore, is *not* the action of the *writing* of the document, but the action of which the document *treats*.

In this example, as in most instances, the author of the work serves only as a recorder, observer, narrator, or analyst of the action or process of which the book treats, and hence for purposes of analysis may be regarded as outside the frame of reference of the formula. But there are instances, of course, in which the author of the book and the agent of the action it records are identical. Such works may be troublesome to analyze because only the product is manifest in the content of the book, the author's contributory act having taken place prior to the writing of the book. The possibility of confusion disappears after more careful examination. Examples showing different types of participation by the author in the action should make this clear.

AGENT	ACT	INSTRUMENTALITY	OBJECT	TIME	SPACE	PRODUCT
Esther Forbes (author)	writes	Imagination Technical skill as writer Knowledge of witchcraft Knowledge of life in 17th cent. Mass.	paper (unimportant in this example)	17th century	Massachusetts	*Mirror for Witches* (novel)

AGENT	ACT	INSTRUMENTALITY	OBJECT	TIME	SPACE	PRODUCT
Wm. Beebe (author)	observes collects assembles writes	Scientific observation Scientific knowledge and skills	paper (unimportant in this example)	Early 20th century	Galapagos Islands	*Galapagos, World's End* (scientific or systematic description)

AGENT	ACT	INSTRUMENTALITY	OBJECT	TIME	SPACE	PRODUCT
Father	interprets	Catholic point of view Scientific data Theological dogma	Theory of evolution		———	*God or Gorilla* (an argument for the rejection of the theory of evolution)

Appendix B
Bibliography on the classified catalog

Ambartsumîan, Z. and others. "O Sistematicheskom Kataloge,"
   Bibliotekar' (October, 1953), pp. 30-35.
Anker, J. T. H. J. "Systematisk Katalogisiering ved Begrebsklas-
   sifikation og Emneregistering," *Nordisk Tidskrift,* XXXIII no. 2
   (1946), pp.57-71.
Barrett, F. T. "Alphabetical and Classified Forms of Catalogues
   Compared," pp.67-71 *in* 2d International Library Conference.
   London, 1897. *Proceedings.* London: The Conference, 1898.
Berthold, A. B. "Future of the Catalog in Research Libraries,"
   College and Research Libraries, VIII (January, 1947), pp.20-22,
   53.
Bishop, W. W. *Practical Handbook of Modern Library Cataloging,*
   2d ed., pp.45-48. Baltimore: Williams & Wilkens Co., 1927.
Bond, H. "Classified versus Dictionary Catalogues," *Library
   Association Record,* II (June, 1900), pp.313-18.
Brown, J. D. and Jast, L. S. "Compilation of Class Lists," *Li-
   brary,* IX (1897), pp.45-69.
Bullen, R. F. "Library Catalogues: Their Effects and Defects,"
   Library Assistant, V (March, 1907), pp.235-39.

Casteele, E. J. van de. "Enhde Beschonwingen ober der Systematischen Catalogue in Wetenschappelrjke Bibliotheken," *Wetensch
Vlaamsch Cong Boek-en Bibliotheckweyen Handelingen,* V (1938),
pp.111-18.

Cole, G. W. "The Future of Cataloguing," *Library Journal,* XV
(1890), pp.172-76.

Cranshaw, J. "The Public and the Catalogue: Dictionary or Classified," *Library Assistant,* XXX (March, 1937), pp.72-78.

Cutter, C. A. "Library Catalogues," pp.526-622 *in* U.S. Bureau of
Education. *Public Libraries in the United States of America.*
Part I. Washington: Government Printing Office, 1876.

Dabrowska, W. "Uwagi w Sprawie Klaryfikacji i Katalogow," *Bib-
liotekary,* XIII (June-July, 1946), pp.134-36. (Title: "Remarks
about Classification and Cataloging.")

Dewey, H. T. "Some Special Aspects of the Classified Catalog,"
pp.114-29 *in* Tauber, M. F., *ed., Subject Analysis of Library
Materials.* New York: Columbia University, 1953.

Diesch, K. "Katalogfragen," *Zentralblatt für Bibliothekswesen,*
LIV (September-October, 1937), pp.428-44.

Dorogutina, E. S. "K Voprossu ob Organizatsii Sistematicheskogo
Kataloga," *Sovetskaiā Bibliografiiā,* no. 4 (1935), pp.113-20.
(Title: "On the Question of the Organization of the Systematic
Catalog.")

Doubleday, W. E. "Class Lists or Dictionary Catalogs," *Library*
IX (1897), pp.179-87.

————. "Dictionary versus Classified Catalogue for Lending
Libraries — The Dictionary Catalogue," *Library Association
Record,* III (October, 1901), pp.521-31.

Doughty, D. W. "Chain Procedure Subject Indexing and Featuring
a Classified Catalogue," *Library Association Record,* LVII
(May, 1955), pp.173-78.

Fisby, N. K. "Subject Index," *Library World,* XLIX (December,
1946), pp.75-77.

Freeman, C. B. "Classified Catalogue: A Plea for Its Abolition
in Public Libraries," *Library Association Record,* XLIV (October, 1942), pp.147-50.

Funnell, H. A. "Sketch of the History of the Classified Catalogue
in the British Isles," *Library World,* XIV (1912), pp.197-200.

Ganley, M. "Some Problems in Cataloging," *Public Libraries,* VI
(1901) pp.139-43.

Garde, P. K. "Apropos of the Last Link Index Entry of the Colon
Classification Code," *Indian Librarian,* II (September-December,
1947), pp.49-55.

Garnett, R. "Public Libraries and Their Catalogs," *Library Journal,* IV (1879), pp.452-53.

Gjelsness, R. "The Classed Catalog versus the Dictionary Catalog," *Library Journal*, LVI (January 1, 1931), pp.18-21.

Grolier, G. de. "Le Catalogue Alphabétique de Sujets," *Revue du Livre et des Bibliothèques*, II (September-October, 1934), pp. 234-44.

Herrick, M. D. "Development of a Classified Catalog for a University Library," *College and Research Libraries*, XIV (October, 1953), pp.418-24.

Hilgenberg, O. C. "Der flächenhafte Realkatalog mit Dezimalklassifikation und Schlagwortregister," *Zentralblatt für Bibliothekswesen*, LXVII (July-August, 1953), pp.254-87; (September-October, 1953), pp.342-57.

Holck, J. "Katalogappartet i Folkebibliotekerne," *Bogens Verden*, XX (March, 1938), pp.67-70.

Holst, H. "Blattkatalog oder Kartothek als Systematischer Bibliothekskatalog," *Zentralblatt für Bibliothekswesen*, LIV (November, 1937), pp.556-64.

Hulme, E. W. "On the Construction of the Subject Catalogue in Scientific and Technical Libraries," *Library Association Record*, III (October, 1901), pp.507-13.

Jast, L. S. "The Class List," *Library*, IX (1897), pp.41-44.

————. "Studies in Library Practice; II. Classified and Annotated Cataloguing Suggestions and Rules. Classified versus Dictionary Cataloguing," *Library World*, I (1899), pp.159-62.

————. "What the Classified Catalog Does," *Library World*, I (1899), pp.213-15.

Jensen, E. A. "Katalogapparatet i Folkebibliotekerne," *Bogens Verden*, XIX (November, 1937), pp.281-86; (December, 1937), pp.325-34.

————. "Svar til fru Struckmann," *Bogens Verden*, XX (June, 1938), pp.149-51.

Kaiser, R. "Die Katalogisierung," III "Der Realkatalog," pp.271-88 *in* Milkan, F., *ed.*, *Handbuch der Bibliothekswissenschaft*. Zweiter Band. Leipzig: Harrassowitz, 1933.

Kelley, G. O. "The Classified Catalog in a Reference Library," *Special Libraries*, XXI (December, 1930), pp.398-402.

Knapp, P. B. "The Subject Catalog in the College Library; the Background of Subject Cataloging," *Library Quarterly*, XIV (1944), pp.108-18, 215-28.

Larned, J. N. "Classification," *Library Journal*, VII (1882), pp.125-30.

Lillie, W. "Merits of the Classified and Dictionary Catalogues," *Library World*, XVII (1914), pp.97-102.

Line, M. B. "Classified Catalogue of Musical Scores; Some Problems," *Library Association Record*, LIV (November, 1952), pp.362-64.

Lowe, E. G. "Subject-Index to the Classified Catalogue," *Library World*, XLIV (July, 1941), pp.3-5.

Lynn, J. J. M. "Future of Cataloging and Classification," *Catholic Library World*, XIII (February, 1942), pp.138-44, 149.

McClelland, E. H. "The Classified Catalogue as a Tool for Research," pp.104-12 *in* A.L.A. Catalogers Section. *Yearbook*, Vol. I, 1929.

McDaniel, C. Classified or Divided Catalog? *A Review and Annotated Bibliography of Critical Discussions*. Master's thesis, Drexel Institute of Technology, 1951. Pp.33.

McDonald, F. "Subject Index to the Classified Catalogue," *Library World*, XLI (June, 1939), pp.254-57.

McDonald, S. "More about the Classified Catalogue," *Library Assistant*, XXXII (April, 1939), pp.101-02.

Mann, Margaret. *Introduction to Cataloging and the Classification of Books*. 2d ed., pp.181-88. Chicago: American Library Association, 1943.

Mills, J. "Chain Indexing and the Classified Catalogue," *Library Association Record*, LVII (April, 1955), pp.141-48.

Neesham, E. W. "Amplified Indexing," *Library World*, XXIV (1921), pp.67-70.

Ohdedar, A. K. "Library Cataloguing by Classified Catalogue Code," *Indian Librarian*, II (June, 1947), pp.22-25.

Palmer, B. I. "Classified Catalogue: A Reply to Mr. C. B. Freeman," *Library Association Record*, XLVI (April, 1944), pp.59-60.

Penfield, H. E. "The J. C. L. Classified Catalogue and Its Subject Index," *The John Crerar Library Quarterly*, V (April-June, 1934), pp.10-15.

Phelps, R. H. "Subject Headings Again," *Library Journal*, LXVI (June 1, 1941), pp.471.

Plant, W. C. "Classified and Dictionary Systems of Cataloguing Compared, with Suggestions for the Adoption of a Combination of Both," *Library Association Record*, I (1899), pp.350-51.

Pollard, A. F. C. and Bradford, S. C. "The Inadequacy of the Alphabetical Subject Index," *ASLIB, Report of Proceedings of the Conferences*, VII (1930), pp.39-52.

Prevost, M. L. "Is Classificatory Approach the Best for Maps?" *Library Journal*, LXXI (January 15, 1946), pp.93-94.

Quinn, J. H. "Dictionary Catalogues versus Classified Catalogues for Public Libraries — The Classified Catalogue," *Library Association Record*, III (October, 1901), pp.514-20.

Rae, W. S. C. "Class Lists," *Library World*, II (1900), pp.298-99.

Rang, B. "Der Frage der Systematik und der Zenordnung der systematischen Kataloge," *Bücherei*, VI (May, 1939), pp. 297-306.

Ranganathan, S. R. *Classified Catalogue Code,* 3d ed. Madras: Madras Library Association, 1951.

——————. *Theory of Library Catalogue.* Madras: Madras Library Association, 1938.

Rider, F. "Alternatives for the Present Dictionary Card Catalog," pp.133-62 *in* Randall, W. M., *ed., Acquisition and Cataloging of Books.* Chicago: University of Chicago Press, 1941.

Robertshaw, W. S. "Classified or the Dictionary Catalogue?" *Librarian,* VI (September, 1915), pp.29-32.

Runge, S. "Die Vereinheittichung der Allgemeingruppen im Systematischen Katalog," *Zentralblatt für Bibliothekswesen,* LI (January-February, 1934), pp.57-71; (March, 1934), pp.146-61.

Rushevskgiã, G. "Oformlenie Sistematicheskogo Katalogo v Massovykh Biblioteckekh," *Bibliotekar',* (August, 1948), pp.26-32. (Title: "Formation of Classed Catalogs in Public Libraries.")

Saraceni Fantini, B. "Catalogo per Sogetto e Catalogo Sistematico," *Accademice e Bibliotecke d'Italia,* X (March-April, 1936), pp. 113-17.

Sauvenier-Goffin, É. "Le Catalogue par matières d'une bibliotheque universitaire," *Archives, Bibliothèques et Musées de Belgique,* XXV no. 1 (1954), pp.57-67.

Sayers, W. C. B. *An Introduction to Library Classification,* 8th ed., pp.180-89. London: Grafton & Co., 1950.

Schwartz, J. "New York Apprentices Library Catalogue," pp.657-60 *in* U.S. Bureau of Education. *Public Libraries in the U. S. of America.* Washington: Government Printing Office, 1876.

Sharp, H. A. *Cataloguing,* 4th ed., pp.23-27. London: Grafton & Co., 1948.

Sivaraman, K. M. "Library Catalogue and Research Work," *Modern Librarian,* V (January, 1935), pp.65-71.

Struckmann, I. "Katalogapparatet i Folkebibliotekerne," *Bogens Verden,* XX (April-May, 1938), pp.109-14.

Surramaniam, D. "Evolution of Classified Catalogue," *Indian Librarian,* IX (June, 1954), pp.17-21.

Taylor, K. T. "Subject Catalogs *vs.* Classified Catalogs," pp.100-13 *in* Tauber, M. F., *ed., Subject Analysis of Library Materials.* New York: Columbia University, 1953.

Taylor, M. S. "The Classified Catalogue and Its Indexes," *Library Assistant,* XXXII (March, 1939), pp.58-63.

Tedder, H. R. "The New Subject-Index of the London Library," *Library Association Record,* XI (1909), pp.476-85.

Thomas, E. C. "Classed Catalogue and the New Classed Catalogue of the German Reichsgericht," *Library Association Monthly Notes,* IV (1883), pp.42-45.

Trebst, Hans. *Studien zu einer Analytischen Sachkatalogisierung.*
Leipzig: Harrassowitz, 1931.

Upton, E. S. "The Adaptability of a Classified Catalogue to a University Library," *Special Libraries,* XXII (January, 1931), pp. 16-17.

Voigt, M. J. "The Development and Use of a Classified Catalog for Periodical Literature in Selected Subject Fields," *Special Libraries,* XXXVII (November, 1946), pp. 285-90.

Vorstius, Joris. *Die Sachkatalogisierung in den Wissenschaftlichen Allgemeinbibliotheken Deutschlands,* pp.10-24. Leipzig: Harrassowitz, 1948.

Willcock, W. J. "Classed Catalogues and Their Indexes," *Library World,* III (1901), pp.261-62.

Zimmerman, E. "Die Sachkatalogisierung an den Deutschen Bibliotheken nach dem Kriege; Ergebnisse einer Umfrage," *Zentralblatt für Bibliothekswesen,* LXIV (July-August, 1950), pp. 246-68.

Index

(*Note:* References in the form, A1:87, refer to sections, numbered paragraphs, and pages in the CODE, pages 87-103.)